## Everything you ever wanted to know about an electric vehicle but were afraid to ask

*All the facts about electric vehicles without any hype or propaganda*

By

P Xavier BSc MSc

Copyright © 2019

ISBN 9781096326106

# Acknowledgements

I'd like to thank Richard McInnes for his invaluable assistance regarding the mechanical sections in this book & also Jim Scutt for his excellent proof reading.

# Introduction

Having read a number of books that claim to teach the reader how to build/install green installations, it became plainly obvious that they all fell into two camps. The first were written by science boffins & are packed with PhD level scientific formulae, which is way beyond the needs or ability of most DIYers. The second set was so brief & contained so little information that they were basically pamphlets padded out with useless & sometimes dangerous information. Neither of these can be of use to the average person. This book is therefore aimed at everyone & imparts practical information to anyone who wishes to learn about the practicalities & economics of installing &/or running an electric vehicle from home. It's not a guide for idiots, but a useful & practical guide for everyone.

This book contains the sections that are relevant to electric vehicles from the book 'DIY home energy solutions' by the same author, where photovoltaic systems, wind turbine energy generating systems, back-up electricity systems, solar water heating, ground sourced hot water & also light tubes are covered in detail. Each of those topic areas have been arranged into three broad groups. Design, installation & maintenance. Therefore, the reader should easily become competent in designing, constructing & running a system that is suitable for their own unique & individual needs. Both here & in 'DIY home energy solutions' all areas have been laid out in plain & simple English, allowing the concepts to be within anyone's grasp, regardless of their academic ability.

# Table of Contents

**ACKNOWLEDGEMENTS** ................................................................ 2
**INTRODUCTION** .......................................................................... 3
**TABLE OF CONTENTS** ............................................................... 4
**NOTES** ........................................................................................... 9
**CHAPTER 1 – THE MOTOR VEHICLE** ...................................... 10
   A BRIEF HISTORY OF THE MOTOR VEHICLE ...................................... 10
   HOW A PETROL ENGINE WORKS – IN A NUTSHELL ........................... 15
   HOW A DIESEL ENGINE WORKS – IN A NUTSHELL ............................ 17
   HOW A MODIFIED DIESEL ENGINE WORKS – IN A NUTSHELL ............ 20
   HOW A HYBRID VEHICLE WORKS – IN A NUTSHELL ......................... 24
      *Power split or series parallel hybrid* ............................ 24
      *Parallel hybrid* ............................................................. 25
      *Mild parallel hybrid* ..................................................... 25
      *Series or serial hybrid* ................................................ 26
      *Plug in hybrid electric vehicle (PHEV)* ....................... 26
   HOW A GAS ENGINE WORKS – IN A NUTSHELL ................................. 27
      *LPG converter & mixer system* ................................... 28
      *LPG vapour phase injection (VPI)* .............................. 28
      *LPG liquid phase injection (LPI)* ................................. 28
      *LPG liquid phase direct injection (LPDI)* ................... 29
   HOW A HYDROGEN ENGINE WORKS – IN A NUTSHELL ...................... 30
      *Polymer exchange membrane fuel cell (PEM)* .......... 31
      *Hydrogen fuelled internal combustion engine* ........... 32
   HOW AN ELECTRIC ENGINE WORKS – IN A NUTSHELL ...................... 33

**CHAPTER 2 – FUELS** ................................................................. 37
   FOSSIL FUELS ................................................................................ 37
   HYDROGEN GAS ............................................................................. 42
   ELECTRICITY .................................................................................. 45

**CHAPTER 3 – ELECTRIC CARS NEED BATTERIES** ................ 50
   BATTERIES ..................................................................................... 50
      *Lead-Acid* ..................................................................... 51
      *Zinc-air fuel cells* ......................................................... 53
      *Sodium–nickel chloride (Zebra)* .................................. 53

*Nickel Cadmium (NiCd or NiCad)* .................................................. *54*
*Nickel-Metal-Hydride (NiMH)* ......................................................... *55*
*Lithium-Ion (Li-Ion)* ........................................................................ *55*
A REFRESHER ON ELECTRICITY ............................................................. 57
BATTERY CHARGING ............................................................................. 59
*Regenerative braking, e-braking or KERS* ..................................... *60*
EVB'S USED IN BEV'S .......................................................................... 60
*Series or parallel* ............................................................................ *62*

## CHAPTER 4 – ELECTRIC CARS NEED ELECTRIC MOTORS............ 66

ELECTRIC MOTORS ............................................................................... 66
*Motor parts* ..................................................................................... *67*
AC MOTORS ........................................................................................ 69
*The synchronous motor* ................................................................. *70*
*Asynchronous or induction motor* ................................................. *71*
*Single phase induction motor* ........................................................ *72*
*Three phase induction motor* ........................................................ *72*
*The AC induction motor & the permanent magnet motor* ............ *73*
DC MOTORS ........................................................................................ 74
*Separately Excited DC Motors (SEDC)* ........................................... *76*
*Permanent Magnet DC Motors (PMDC)* ........................................ *76*
*Shunt Wound DC Motor (SWDM)* .................................................. *77*
*Series Wound DC Motor (SWDM)* .................................................. *77*
*Compound Wound DC Motor (CWDM)* .......................................... *77*
SERIES OR PARALLEL AGAIN .................................................................. 78
*Series drivetrains* ........................................................................... *79*
*Parallel drivetrains* ........................................................................ *79*
*Series/Parallel drivetrains* ............................................................. *80*
DRIVETRAIN INERTIA ............................................................................. 80

## CHAPTER 5 – AC, DC & ELECTRONICS ........................................... 82

AC/DC ............................................................................................... 82
ELECTRONICS ...................................................................................... 86
*Rectifier* .......................................................................................... *86*
*Inverter* ........................................................................................... *87*
*Converter* ....................................................................................... *87*
*Tandem unit* ................................................................................... *87*
*Battery Management System (BMS)* ............................................. *88*
*Controller* ....................................................................................... *89*

## CHAPTER 6 – CABLES, CONNECTIONS & POWER .......................... 90

CHARGE MODES .................................................................................. 91
*Mode 1* ........................................................................................... *91*
*Mode 2* ........................................................................................... *91*
*Mode 3* ........................................................................................... *92*
*Mode 4* ........................................................................................... *92*
CHARGING CABLES & THEIR PLUGS ........................................................ 93
*Type 1 - J1772 (Yazaki connector)* ................................................. *94*

    *Rapid charging CHAdeMO* ............................................................... *95*
    *Type 2 – IEC62196 (Mennekes connector)* ..................................... *96*
    *CCS Combo* ..................................................................................... *97*
    *The trouble with Tesla* ..................................................................... *98*
  SIMPLIFIED CHARGING ............................................................................ *99*
    *Slow charging (3kW)* ....................................................................... *99*
    *Fast charging (7-22kW)* ................................................................. *100*
    *Rapid AC charging (up to 43kW)* .................................................. *100*
    *Rapid DC charging (up to 50kW)* .................................................. *101*
    *A note on the LEAF* ...................................................................... *101*
  CURRENT DEVELOPMENTS IN BATTERY TECHNOLOGIES ........................... *102*
    *Magnesium batteries* .................................................................... *103*
    *Paper-polymer batteries* ............................................................... *103*
    *Silicon-based batteries* ................................................................. *103*
    *Room-temperature sodium sulfur (RT-NaS) batteries* ................... *104*
    *Nickel-zinc batteries* ..................................................................... *104*
    *Potassium-ion batteries* ................................................................ *104*
    *Salt-water batteries* ....................................................................... *104*
    *Proton batteries* ............................................................................ *105*
    *Aluminium-ion batteries* ................................................................ *105*
  CURRENT DEVELOPMENTS IN BATTERY CHARGING TECHNOLOGIES ........... *105*
    *Ultra fast charging* ........................................................................ *106*
    *Inductive charging* ........................................................................ *106*
  THE CHARGING NETWORK ..................................................................... *108*
    *UK* .................................................................................................. *108*
    *EEC* ............................................................................................... *110*
    *Canada* .......................................................................................... *111*
    *USA* ............................................................................................... *112*
    *South America* .............................................................................. *112*
    *Australia* ........................................................................................ *112*
    *New Zealand* ................................................................................. *113*
    *Japan* ............................................................................................ *113*
    *China* ............................................................................................. *113*
    *Singapore* ...................................................................................... *113*

**CHAPTER 7 – HIDDEN COSTS** ............................................................ **114**

  INSURANCE COSTS ............................................................................... *114*
  BATTERY LEASE .................................................................................... *116*
  PUBLIC CHARGING ................................................................................ *118*
  PRIVATE CHARGING .............................................................................. *123*
  ENVIRONMENTAL COSTS ....................................................................... *124*
    *Carbon credits* .............................................................................. *124*
    *Nickel* ............................................................................................ *125*
    *Cobalt* ........................................................................................... *126*
    *Lithium* .......................................................................................... *126*
    *$CO_2$ emissions* ........................................................................ *127*
  HEALTH COSTS ..................................................................................... *128*
    *Electromagnetic radiation* ............................................................. *129*

*Particulate matter* ................................................................ *131*
  *Pedestrian casualties* ......................................................... *131*
  *Fire* ......................................................................................... *132*
  *Electrocution* ...................................................................... *133*
  THE TAXPAYER ............................................................................ 133

**CHAPTER 8 – GRANTS & INITIATIVES** ........................................... **135**
  UK ............................................................................................... 135
    *Category 1 vehicles* .............................................................. *135*
    *Category 1 cars* .................................................................... *136*
    *Category 1 vans* ................................................................... *136*
    *Category 1 motorbikes* ........................................................ *137*
    *Category 1 mopeds* ............................................................. *137*
    *Category 1 taxis* ................................................................... *137*
    *Category 2 vehicles* ............................................................. *138*
    *Category 3 vehicles* ............................................................. *138*
    *Electric vehicle homecharge scheme (EVHS)* ..................... *139*
    *Workplace charging schemes* ............................................. *140*
    *On street parking schemes* ................................................. *141*
    *London congestion charge exemption* ................................ *142*
    *London toxicity charge* ....................................................... *144*
    *London ultra low emission zone exemption* ....................... *144*
    *Road tax exemption* ............................................................ *146*
    *Salary sacrifice* .................................................................... *147*
    *Reduction in BiK tax for company car drivers* ................... *148*
    *100% First year allowance (FYA)* ....................................... *149*
    *Approved mileage allowance payments (AMAPs)* .............. *149*
  EEC ............................................................................................. 150
    *Austria* ................................................................................. *150*
    *Belgium* ................................................................................ *151*
    *Bulgaria* ................................................................................ *151*
    *Cyprus* .................................................................................. *151*
    *Czech Republic* .................................................................... *152*
    *Denmark* .............................................................................. *152*
    *Estonia* ................................................................................. *152*
    *Finland* ................................................................................. *152*
    *France* .................................................................................. *152*
    *Germany* .............................................................................. *154*
    *Greece* ................................................................................. *155*
    *Hungary* ............................................................................... *155*
    *Iceland* ................................................................................. *156*
    *Ireland* .................................................................................. *156*
    *Italy* ...................................................................................... *156*
    *Latvia* ................................................................................... *157*
    *Luxembourg* ........................................................................ *157*
    *Monaco* ................................................................................ *157*
    *Netherlands* ......................................................................... *158*
    *Norway* ................................................................................ *158*

  *Portugal* ............................................................................ *159*
  *Romania* ........................................................................... *159*
  *Spain*.................................................................................. *160*
  *Sweden*............................................................................. *160*
 CANADA.................................................................................. 161
 USA........................................................................................ 163
 AUSTRALIA............................................................................. 164
 JAPAN .................................................................................... 164
 CHINA..................................................................................... 165

**CHAPTER 9 – MAINTENANCE** ........................................................ **166**

 MINOR MAINTENANCE ............................................................... 167
  *Brakes* ............................................................................... *167*
  *Tyres*.................................................................................. *167*
  *Coolant system* ................................................................. *168*
  *Wiper blades*..................................................................... *168*
  *Headlamps & bulbs* ......................................................... *168*
  *Fluids* ................................................................................ *169*
  *Motor factor parts* ............................................................ *169*
 MAJOR MAINTENANCE .............................................................. 170
  *Battery system*.................................................................. *170*
  *Servicing*........................................................................... *171*
 THE UK MOT ......................................................................... 172
 MAINTENANCE & SERVICE COSTS .............................................. 174

**TABLE OF ILLUSTRATIONS** ............................................................ **176**

**ABOUT THE AUTHOR** .................................................................... **177**

# Notes

This work is by the author & as such, all copyright belongs to the author. You are not permitted to copy any text or images without the authors express permission.

Some of the images in this book are created by the book's author, others are either in the public domain or individually credited to their respective creator &/or copyright owner. Any other images are from sources where they are copyright free.

This work is fully referenced to aid the reader in any future studies. That being said, internet references have been provided to aid study as most individuals do not have huge libraries at their disposal. It is far easier to research material online than to go through the expense of ordering specific books at a public lending library.

# Chapter 1 – **The motor vehicle**

The reason you are reading this book is because either you have an interest in electric vehicles, considering purchasing an electric vehicle or wish to future proof your transport arrangements for the coming years as it is highly likely that traditional petrol/diesel vehicles will become outlawed.

Therefore, it would be advantageous to understand where these electric vehicles have come from & why. Also, it would be expedient to explore how these electric vehicles differ from traditional petrol/diesel vehicles & how they work. Clearly even with a basic level of comprehension on electric vehicles, this will enable the reader to cut through any misleading advertising &/or inappropriate sales advice at a dealership.

## A brief history of the motor vehicle

The internal combustion engine is acknowledged to have been invented in 1861 in Germany by Nikolaus August Otto[1]. At that time Otto was enhancing an engine built in France by Jean Joseph Etienne Lenoir which used a gas engine. Otto worked to develop it as a liquid fuel (petrol) engine & what he created became known as the Otto engine & the principles he developed in his engine (known as 'four stroke') are still used to this day in petrol engines.

---

[1] https://en.wikipedia.org/wiki/Nikolaus_Otto - 26/02/2019

The modern production car is acknowledged to have been invented in 1886 by Karl Benz[2], who patented his Benz Patent-Motorwagon[3]. This was given the German patent number 37435 on 29th January 1886 (as this was the date he first applied for the patent). It is acknowledged to be the first as it was designed to generate & be propelled under its own power, not simply a motorised stage coach or horse carriage, & this is why Karl Benz was granted his patent & is now universally regarded as the inventor of the motor car.

Approximately 25 of those first Patent-Motorwagens were subsequently built between 1886 & 1893. They were each powered by his Benz 954 cc single-cylinder, four stroke engine which cranked out (500w) 2/3 horse power at 250 rpm when fitted to the rear of his three wheeled vehicle. Benz later went on to develop & improve his Motorwagon. First with the model 2 which had a (1.1kw) 1.5 horse power engine, then again with the model 3, which boasted (1.5kw) 2 horse power engine, which gave the model 3 a top speed of 10mph (16kph).

Before the Motorwagen, Benz was designing & producing stationary engines & invented many components that are still used in modern vehicles. Ignition using a battery, spark plugs, carburettor, gear shift & the water filled radiator were all Benz's own designs.

Following Benz's trailblazing; Henry Ford in the USA developed the Model T for the American masses in 1908 under the company name of the Ford Motor Company & became famous for pioneering the production line.
Before Karl Benz & Henry Ford, the evolution of the car went through many stages.

---

[2] https://en.wikipedia.org/wiki/Karl_Benz - 24/02/2019

[3] https://en.wikipedia.org/wiki/Benz_Patent-Motorwagen - 24/02/2019

In China in 1672 Ferdinand Verbiest built a steam powered vehicle, but it was not big enough to carry a human, but was said to be the first working steam powered vehicle. In France, 1769, Nicolas-Joseph Cugnot created a steam powered vehicle that was capable of transporting humans. He called it a *fardier à vapeur* (steam dray) & he designed it as an experimental steam-driven artillery tractor. Then in 1784 in Redruth, UK, William Murdoch built a working model of a steam carriage. By 1801 in Camborne, UK, Richard Trevithick was running a full sized vehicle. Following this, several other steam powered vehicles were introduced onto the roads in the UK, but this caused such distress to the public that the UK government legislated in 1865 that all self propelled vehicles must have a man walking in front waving a red flag & blowing a horn so as to warn the public of the approaching vehicle. In 1896 this law was repealed.

In 1808 François Isaac de Rivaz created a vehicle powered by an internal combustion engine which was fuelled by hydrogen. In Prague in 1816, Josef Bozek built an oil-fired steam car. By 1828, a Hugarian called Ányos Jedlik invented a basic electric motor then used it to power a small model vehicle. In Vermont USA in 1834, Thomas Davenport designed a DC electric motor & also used it in a small model vehicle. The following year in the Netherlands, Professor Sibrandus Stratingh of Groningen created a small scale electric vehicle. Then by 1838 Robert Davidson built an electric locomotive that could achieve 4mph.

In 1892, Rudolph Diesel had been granted a patent for his New Rational Combustion Engine. Then by 1897 he had created the first diesel engine.

It should be clear that the development of motor vehicles was widely dispersed, over a wide timescale & they used various power sources. This was due to the fact that the inventors utilised the power sources that they had to hand. Steam, electric & petrol vehicles were all competing head to head for dominance in this fast emerging market. It was not until the network of petrol filling stations was built until after 1910 when the Ford Model T became popular & so too was the need for petrol, that the petrol fuelled internal combustion engine achieved dominance over its competitors. Until then, petrol was only obtainable from chemist shops. When Karl Benz's wife undertook the first production car long distance trip in 1888, she had to plan her journey to pass numerous chemist shops en-route just to source petrol.

Enhancements were then developed to the petrol fed internal combustion engine, the driveability & safety of the vehicle quickly followed. WWI was a particularly active time for innovation, but it was only during the oil crisis of 1973 when the focus started to move into other technologies. Interestingly, since 1892, the diesel engine was being developed alongside petrol & now 20% of all passenger cars globally are diesel powered, with Europe having 47% of its passenger cars being diesel powered. The uptake of diesel powered vehicles is currently still increasing globally, most prominently in India, Japan & South Korea.

More recently, both the UK & the EEC governments have signed up to reducing greenhouse gas emissions, they have therefore announced that they intend to legislate to outlaw the sale of all new diesel & petrol vehicles by 2040[4]. This has predictably caused problems for car manufacturers, car mechanics & even members of the public who wish to purchase a new vehicle, as a credible replacement to the internal combustion engine does not yet exist.

---

[4] https://www.theguardian.com/politics/2017/jul/25/britain-to-ban-sale-of-all-diesel-and-petrol-cars-and-vans-from-2040- 24/02/2019

The reason why petrol/diesel power has powered the world's vehicles since Benz's Motorwagon until now is simple. Petrol/diesel (any oil derived fuel) has more extractable energy per kilo than any other commonly available fuel source.

The simple graph in figure 1 demonstrates this simple fact while comparing it to various other power sources.
You should be aware of the cost of petrol or diesel at the forecourt if you drive a vehicle. At the time of writing this book, the cost on the UK for diesel is £1.22p per litre & petrol being £1.16p per litre. The equivalent amount of hydrogen currently costs £9.99p, therefore despite hydrogen containing three times more extractable mega joules per kilo making it more energy dense, it is currently 8.6 times more expensive than petrol, which does not allow it to be an economically viable alternative to petrochemical fuels.

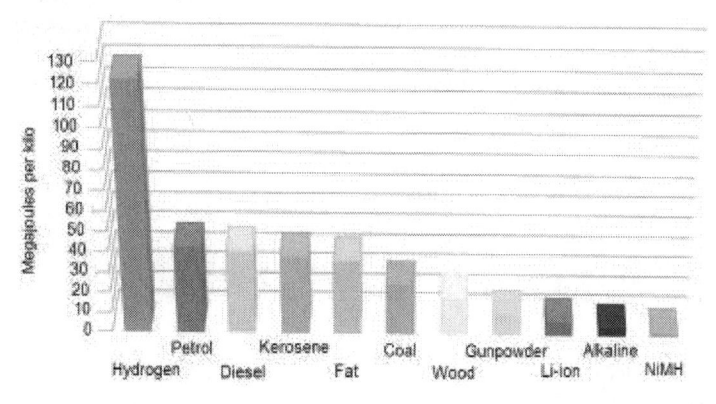

*Figure 1 Extractable energy from various fuels per kilo (P Xavier © 2019)*

However, despite the low cost of petrol/diesel fuels & the thousands of gradual enhancements, developments to both the internal combustion engine & motor vehicles in general since Otto in 1861, the development focus has now shifted away from petrochemical powered vehicles, so once again there is a development race in the field of motor vehicles.

This time, the race is on to find a suitable replacement for the petrol/diesel engine, but until a credible replacement is found & any associated infrastructure built to support it, the majority of the vehicles on the road will remain to be either petrol or diesel powered. It will therefore be advantageous to understand exactly how these engines work, to understand & compare them to the emerging alternatives.

However, as steam/coal powered vehicles are not carbon neutral, it is unlikely that they will see a resurgence, therefore both those options can be omitted from this study.

## How a petrol engine works – in a nutshell

At the heart of the petrol powered vehicle is the internal combustion engine. In the heart of that engine are cylinders. There could be 2, 4, 6, 8, 10 or even 12 cylinders, but typically there are 4, 6 or 8. Inside these cylinders is where aerated petrol is fed & this is where it is made to explode (internal combustion). These cylinders are sealed, but at the top they have a spark plug & two inlets (one to allow the aerated petrol in, the other to allow the exhaust gas out). These inlets can therefore be seen as gates. One in, one out & they operate in sequence. One gate opens to let in the aerated petrol. Then a spark from the spark plug then causes the aerated petrol to explode inside the cylinder. The second gate then opens & the hot gas is expelled out.

When the fuel is exploding inside the cylinder, the only direction it can travel is downwards, pushing a very tight fitting piston that is fitted inside the cylinder. The piston is therefore pushed downwards, to the bottom of the cylinder. That piston is attached to the crankshaft by a con-rod & therefore that downward movement is what ultimately moves the crankshaft which powers the vehicle as the downward movement is translated into torque.

This all operates in the same controlled sequence, in what is known as four strokes.

Stroke 1. **Intake**, as the piston is travelling down the cylinder, it creates a vacuum & this allows the air/petrol mixture to be introduced through the inward gate valve.

Stroke 2. **Compression**, the inlet valve closes & the piston then travels back up, compressing the air/petrol mixture (making it highly flammable) inside the cylinder. When the piston reaches the top of the cylinder the spark plug is fired to create a spark inside the chamber.

Stroke 3. **Power**, the aerated petrol then ignites & this mini explosion pushes the piston back down again, thus turning the crankshaft through the con-rod which connects them both.

Stroke 4. **Exhaust**, the outlet valve then opens & as the crankshaft continues to turn, it pushes the piston back up again & this action pushes the hot gas that remains after the explosion, out of the cylinder then down the exhaust. The cycle then repeats itself again & again.

The power from the engine is transmitted through the clutch & the gear box to the rear axle via a crank shaft. Because the rear axle moves up & down due to the suspension, there are splines fitted to the crank shaft that slide in & out of the gear box to compensate for any movement. Universal joints are also fitted on the crank shaft at each end to ensure that the power is delivered regardless to what angle the crank shaft happens to be at. The joint between the crank shaft & the rear axle is fitted with a differential. This then transmits the torque to the wheels via half shafts. The gears are controlled by the driver, as is the accelerator pedal. The accelerator pedal just lets more fuel & air into the engine, which results in greater power.

There is however one issue with the four stroke sequence. That is, power is only being provided on the 3rd stroke. To overcome this issue, four cylinders are generally used together & in sequence. Therefore if cylinder 1, is on stroke 1, cylinder 2 is on stroke 2, cylinder 3 is on stroke 3 & cylinder 4 is on stroke 4. Power is therefore provided on every stroke from one or other of the cylinders & there is therefore no loss of power.

If a simpler or more detailed explanation is required, there are numerous internet sites that give splendid explanations. Many of these sites also use diagrams & videos. A simple internet search will reveal thousands.

## How a diesel engine works – in a nutshell

The modern diesel engine is also an internal combustion engine, but differs from the petrol engine slightly. They are also far simpler which means they are more robust & as a result tend to break down far less than a petrol engine. Firstly, in the diesel engine, it is air that is drawn into the cylinder, not an air-fuel mixture like in the petrol engine. The air in the cylinder is then compressed to between 14 to 25 times its original volume (the petrol engine only compresses the air-fuel mixture about 10 times its original volume).

Compressing any gas always results in an increase in temperature. In the diesel engine, the compressed air needs to achieve a temperature which is a minimum of 500°C. There are glow plugs to aid this process, not spark plugs which are only found in petrol engines. The diesel fuel is then injected into the cylinder where it is ignited by the hot air. The resulting explosion then pushes the piston down just like it would in the petrol engine. When the piston returns up the cylinder, it expels the hot gas in the same method as in the petrol engine.

That piston is attached to the crankshaft by a rod & therefore that downward movement is what ultimately moves the crankshaft. The glow plugs are only present to help warm the air when the engine is cold.

This all operates in the same controlled sequence, in what is known as four strokes.

Stroke 1, **Intake**, air is drawn into the cylinder through the intake valve as the cylinder is drawn down.

Stroke 2, **Compression**, the intake valve closes & the piston moves upwards compressing the air & heating it to at least 500°C. A small amount of diesel fuel is injected into the cylinder where it spontaneously ignites & therefore explodes.

Stroke 3. **Power**, the resulting explosion pushes the piston back down again, thus turning the crankshaft through the con-rod which connects them both.

Stroke 4. **Exhaust**, the outlet valve then opens & as the crankshaft continues to turn, it pushes the piston back up again & this action pushes the hot gas that remains after the explosion, out of the cylinder then down the exhaust. The cycle then repeats itself again & again.

As this is a similar four stroke sequence as was seen in the petrol engine, it has the same downside. That is, power is only provided on the 3rd stroke. Again, to overcome this issue, four cylinders are generally used together & in sequence. Therefore if cylinder 1, is on stroke 1, cylinder 2 is on stroke 2, cylinder 3 is on stroke 3 & cylinder 4 is on stroke 4. Power is therefore provided on every stroke from one or other of the cylinders & the result is no loss of power. Typically, a diesel engine has 2, 4 or 6 cylinders, but the most common configuration is 4.

Even though there is very little difference between the petrol & diesel engines, the diesel engine actually works out to be approximately 40% more efficient, therefore 40% more miles can be travelled in a diesel vehicle than a petrol vehicle using the same volume of fuel. The diesel engine achieves this due to numerous factors.

Firstly, Carnot's rule[5] states that the efficiency of an engine is dependant on the difference between the highest & lowest temperatures in which it operates, therefore if the diesel engine is very hot, or if the external air temperature is very low, then the difference between the two is high & therefore it is more efficient.

Secondly, because of the simplistic design of the diesel engine, it allows the fuel to achieve a higher temperature & therefore removes the need for any spark plugs. The higher temperature also results in a higher percentage of the fuel burning & as a result it releases a greater amount of energy. Thirdly, as the design allows for a higher percentage of power output, the engine therefore operates at a lower output ratio when compared to the petrol engine. Therefore the petrol engine will burn more fuel than the diesel to achieve a comparable power output.

Fourthly, diesel fuel contains more energy than petrol, therefore again less fuel is needed. Finally, diesel fuel also acts as a lubricant, allowing a diesel engine operate with less friction & this results in a longer lifespan for the engine components & less overall maintenance. A diesel engine is not throttled like a petrol engine; therefore the amount of air drawn in at any engine speed is always constant. The engine speed is regulated by the amount of fuel injected into the cylinder. The more fuel injected into the cylinder, the larger the resultant explosion & therefore more power is produced.

---

[5] https://en.wikipedia.org/wiki/Carnot%27s_theorem_(thermodynamics) – 02/03/2019

The accelerator pedal is therefore connected to the metering unit of the engine injection system rather than to the air intake flap which is found in a petrol engine.

Diesel engines produce more power than a petrol equivalent, but operate more slowly. They are also heavier. They are therefore more suited for pulling power, not speed. This is why there are no diesel powered racing cars. Manufacturers therefore tend to add turbochargers to modern diesel engines, in an attempt to boost the performance.

If a simpler or more detailed explanation is required, there are numerous internet sites that give excellent explanations. Many of these sites also use diagrams & videos. A simple internet search will reveal thousands.

## How a modified diesel engine works – in a nutshell

A modified diesel engine works in exactly the same way as a regular diesel engine except it uses alternative fuels rather than regular diesel.

Provided a fuel will burn at the temperature that is present in the engine, then any older type of diesel engine can be powered by that fuel. After all, when Rudolph Diesel first unveiled his diesel engine at the Worlds Fair in Paris in 1900, it was running on peanut oil. Since then, many different types of fuel have been used to power a modified diesel. For example, sunflower oil, coconut oil, cottonseed oil, paraffin, turpentine, coal dust & even buttermilk have all been used (the list is endless).

However, modern diesel engines were never designed to run on alternative fuels, therefore carbon deposits can build up within the engine & the whole engine can also suffer from excessive wear.

Despite the numerous problems that can be encountered by burning non-diesel fuels, there are useable alternatives & useable methods available. The main problem encountered with the alternatives is the viscosity of the fuel. That is, if it is too thick or sticky then problems will be encountered. This is because when the fuel enters a cylinder, it does so through an injector. This injector acts very much like an aerosol spray & it sprays the fuel as a fine mist. It is therefore very easy to block the injector if the viscosity of the fuel is not correct. Any fuel used must therefore be altered to have a viscosity akin to diesel. There are two methods to achieve this. The first is to chemically treat an oil to ensure it has the correct viscosity (this is what biodiesel is – vegetable oil that has been treated to have similar properties to diesel oil).

The second option is to heat an oil to reduce the viscosity until it is similar to diesel. One of the fuels that could be utilised is waste cooking oil (WVO), but the main problem with using WVO is that it often contains cooking waste & even sometimes water. It therefore needs to be filtered to clean the oil before starting any modifications. WVO also has a different viscosity to regular diesel (RDO) & biodiesel (BDO); therefore the diesel engine can not run with this oil straight after filtration. Biodiesel will run without any modification because it has already been chemically treated to make its viscosity the same as RDO. Straight vegetable oil (SVO) also needs to be treated to make it the same viscosity as RDO.

To make filtered WVO & SVO the same viscosity as RDO, it needs to be heated to achieve the desired level of viscosity which is the same viscosity as RDO. Most individuals who run their vehicles from WVO & SVO use this method. They have two tanks in their vehicle, one for WVO/SVO with a heating element & another for RDO.

When the WVO/SVO reaches the desired viscosity, they switch from the RDO fuel tank to the WVO/SVO fuel tank. This involves fitting sensors to the WVO/SVO tank & also the engine so that the driver will know when each of the elements are at the correct temperature & ready to switch. When they are the correct temperature, the fuel feed can then switch from the RDO tank to the WVO/SVO tank.

However, before switching off the engine, the fuel feed must be switched back to the RDO tank & feed for a short while. If this does not happen, any un-burnt WVO/SVO within the engine, or the feed pipes between the engine & the tank will quickly start to revert to its original viscous state. This will result in sticky oil in the engine & the pipework, which could be impossible to remove, thereby killing the engine. To better understand this, imagine a cup of liquid fat that has been placed into your fridge. It will not take long before it becomes solid.

Alternatively, the WVO & SVO can be treated by a process called transesterification, a fairly simple process that uses lye to remove the coagulating properties from the pre cleaned oils. The by product of biodiesel processing is just glycerine, which is used in soaps & other harmless products. Therefore this process will need to be undertaken before the oil is placed in the fuel tank. Most people who use this method undertake the entire process it in their garage or an outbuilding.

Because the majority of diesel engines/generators use an injector pump to feed the fuel into the cylinder, this is where the main viscosity problem occurs. Older diesel generators used a positive displacement fuel pump which supplied fuel continuously to the injectors; therefore the viscosity of the fuel was never a problem. Theoretically, if new diesel engines were to be manufactured with positive displacement fuel pumps, then it would be possible to run pre cleaned WVO, RDO, SVO & BDO without any further modification to the oils, or needing to pre heat it.

Currently, many restaurants & café's are happy for people to remove their WVO either for free or for a small charge as they have to pay for someone to remove it. Therefore there is a clean free (or low cost) energy source that can be utilised to power your vehicle. Also, this fuel source is carbon neutral (as it does not emit any more carbon than it absorbed when it was growing as a plant), The exhaust emissions are cleaner than RDO as it is made from renewable sources, WVO can be obtained locally to you as there will be local restaurants or café's near to you & it will stop the chance of this oil ending up in landfill.

Currently this source of oil is untaxed; therefore the government is keeping very quiet about it rather than promoting it as a clean energy source. There may however come a pointing time when the government decides to tax it. Until they do, it makes excellent fiscal sense to utilise it.

Most armed forces used to use a type of modified diesel engine in their vehicles. They wish to have the ability to use various fuels because in a time of war as there may be difficulties in getting one sort of fuel or another. Many of these vehicles have now been superseded & replaced by diesel powered engines, but the Russian army still use multi-fuel engines in the majority of their vehicles. The reason that these engines were superseded everywhere else was due to their design.

As most engines are designed to perform well for a particular fuel, these had design compromises which allowed them to run on many alternatives. This left these engines being underpowered & sluggish. They burn diesel poorly & are very smokey.

If a simpler or more detailed explanation is required on modified diesel engines, there are numerous internet sites that give wonderful explanations. Many of these sites also use diagrams & videos. A simple internet search will reveal thousands.

# How a hybrid vehicle works – in a nutshell

There are numerous types of hybrid vehicles on the market & the definition of a hybrid vehicle is one that it uses two or more distinct types of power. For example, a typical WWII submarine used a diesel engine whilst at the surface to power its functions & this switched over to running under battery power whilst being submerged. Therefore an old submarine can be classed as a hybrid vehicle.

In the case of a road vehicle, it would be combining either a petrol engine with an electric motor, or a diesel engine with an electric motor. The concept behind this is that in theory, the hybrid could use less petrol/diesel fuel & as a result emit fewer pollutants. This is also based on the theory that different motors operate more efficiently at different speeds. A classic example for this is the power split hybrid.

## Power split or series parallel hybrid

This is the most common type of hybrid, which was detailed a few pages ago. To refresh your memory, here are the characteristics again.

The concept behind this is that in theory, this hybrid could use less petrol/diesel fuel & as a result emit fewer pollutants. This is based on the theory that different motors operate more efficiently at different speeds. For example, the electric engine operates efficiently producing torque; therefore it is used for speeds between 0 – 15mph. The petrol or diesel engine will operate more efficiently when maintaining a higher consistent speed, such as travelling down a motorway. Both therefore will therefore operate at speeds that allow them to function within their preferred operating window. In addition to this, both motors can even be used together when needed, such as during heavy acceleration, where the electric motor will engage to assist the petrol/diesel engine by delivering some power.

The petrol/diesel engine will therefore need to work less hard. This clever use of energy efficiency should therefore translate into better fuel efficiency.

In short, the electric motor in this variant aids the petrol/diesel motor by operating in the range that the petrol/diesel motor is most inefficient. Also, it adds additional power when required. The majority of the 'hybrid' vehicles that are commercially available fall into this type of hybrid, but there are others.

## Parallel hybrid

The parallel hybrid is what was described earlier. That is an electric motor coupled with either a petrol or diesel engine. They can work independently or together as previously described. Typically in a parallel hybrid, the petrol or diesel engine, the electric motor & the gear box are coupled by automatically controlled clutches. During electric driving the clutch between the internal combustion engine is in the open position while the clutch to the gear box is engaged. While in combustion mode the engine & motor run at the same speed.

## Mild parallel hybrid

These variants tend to use a small compact electric motor which are generally less than 20kw which provides auto stop/start, auto power assist during acceleration & generates power during braking which is stored in the battery.

## Series or serial hybrid

In this type of hybrid, the vehicle is driven by an electric motor & therefore it operates as an electric vehicle. However, it also has a conventional petrol or diesel engine which is tuned up to act as a generator for the electric motor when there is insufficient power in the batteries to power the electric motor. There is therefore no physical connection between the conventional motor & the wheels; it is driven solely by the electric motor.

This type of vehicle has also been called 'extended range electric vehicles' (EREV), 'range extended electric vehicles' (REEV) & 'electric vehicle extended range' (EVER). These types of 'hybrids' can either require to be charged up by being plugged into a suitable electric socket to charge up the batteries, or for the batteries to just act as a buffer & therefore need to have the conventional engine to run constantly (when the vehicle is being used) to supply power to the electric motor. This is a typical arrangement commonly seen in diesel/electric train locomotives & also in ships. It is not a new development as it was a system invented & utilised by Ferdinand Porsche in the early 20th century. He called it 'system mixt' & used a wheel hub motor on each of the front wheels which were both powered by a separate motor. His Lohner-Porsche Mixte Hybrid used this system & proved to be very successful; it set several speed records.

The next designation for the hybrid is very similar to the series/serial hybrid.

## Plug in hybrid electric vehicle (PHEV)

This type of hybrid is much the same as the series hybrid, except that it just has a greater electrical storage capacity in the form of lithium-ion batteries.

In all of these vehicles, where power is delivered or derived from a mixture of sources. The manufacturers now use the term 'drive-train' rather than 'engine'. This is purely a marketing gimmick, as it sounds like they are not using a polluting petrol or diesel engine in their car & therefore implies that it has 'green credentials'.

Some people also consider vehicles that use two distinct power sources that power the same engine to be 'hybrids', although 'dual fuelled' would be a better definition. For instance some petrol derived engines can use petrol, ethanol, methanol, bio-butanol & any combination of these mixed in the same fuel tank as they are very similar fuels.

However, liquefied petroleum gas (LPG) & natural gas (NG) are completely different to petrol so can not use the same fuel tank. However, by using separate fuel systems as was seen in the modified diesel example, it would be possible to seamlessly switch between petrol & LPG when the engine is running. It is even possible to use just LPG if petrol is scarce, or just petrol if LPG is scarce. As LPG is currently seven times cheaper than petrol, running a petrol car with LPG currently makes fiscal sense.

## How a gas engine works – in a nutshell

The gas used to power a vehicle is liquefied petroleum gas (LPG). It is a mixture of propane & butane, propane or butane. It is known as autogas in the USA (because the word 'gas' is used there as an abbreviation of gasoline), In Italy & France it is known as GPL (*gas di petrolio liquefatto* & *gaz de pétrole liquéfié*). In Spain they call it GLP (*gas licuado del petróleo*). Any unmodified petrol engine can be used to run on LPG because it is usually just the fuel feeding into the engine that changes, not the engine.

All that is needed is a separate fuel system & feed system, along with the associated electronic controls that will allow the fuel system to switch over from petrol to LPG or vice versa at the flick of a switch & therefore it is the vehicle driver who decides which fuel to use & when to use it. This switch over can even happen when the vehicle is speeding down a motorway.

There are four main types of conversion systems for a petrol engine.

## LPG converter & mixer system

It is the oldest of the systems available & the LPG converts into a vapour & is then mixed with air before going into the inlet manifold.

## LPG vapour phase injection (VPI)

This system uses a converter & mixer system where gas exits the converter under pressure & is then injected into the intake manifold. The electrically controlled injectors improve the metering of fuel going into the engine which improves fuel economy & the resultant power output as well as reducing the emissions.

This system has proven to be the most popular system in recent years.

## LPG liquid phase injection (LPI)

This system injects the liquid fuel directly into the intake manifold through a set of liquid LPG injectors. It is here where it vaporises. The vaporising causes cooling to the air & therefore increases the density of the intake air. This results in a large increase in power output, improves fuel economy & has even lower emissions, when compared to the VPI system.

## LPG liquid phase direct injection (LPDI)

This is the most advanced LPG system, where LPG is injected directly into cylinder where it instantly vaporises & cools both the cylinder & the fuel/air mixture within it during the compression stroke. This provides even further performance & emission improvements as the cooling increases the density of the air-fuel mixture. The whole system is controlled with an Electronic Control Unit (ECU) which controls each of the components in the injection system & the injectors themselves. This optimises both the flow & LPG injection timing because the ECU is tuned to the specific vehicle & the individual engine.

The benefits for using one of the LPG systems is that it is a cleaner fuel & therefore produces less carbon dioxide emissions than a petrol fuelled system. Diesel engine carbon dioxide emissions are 29.2% higher than LPG whilst petrol is 26.8% higher than LPG, in addition to this, LPG fuelled engines produce 95% less ozone & smog causing nitrogen oxide than a diesel engine.

Engine wear is also reduced as when petrol passes over the oil rings (fitted around the piston), it washes out the lubricant film from the upper cylinder surface. This causes a lack of lubricant which increases wear & tear. Therefore the life of petrol engine is far less than it could be when compared to the longevity of a LPG powered engine. This is because LPG does not remove the lubricant film; hence the life of LPG powered engine is increased by 50%.

The MPG of LPG is also 10% greater than can be achieved with petrol; therefore a higher 10% MPG will result from every tank of LPG fuel. Also, as stated earlier, LPG is currently seven times cheaper than petrol, therefore running a petrol car with LPG as a fuel currently makes fiscal sense.

# How a hydrogen engine works – in a nutshell

In the previous examples of how various engines work, either a fuel is burnt so that it pushes pistons that in turn, rotate a crankshaft to turn the wheels, or in electric vehicles an electric motor turns the wheels. The hybrids use a combination of both & can therefore switch between the two. The hydrogen engine is a little strange. It does not burn a fossil fuel, or use a battery because hydrogen is not a fuel, nor is it electricity.

Hydrogen it is the most simple, common & abundant element in the universe. It is estimated that three quarters of the universe is actually made from hydrogen. However, it is hidden inside other elements so it needs a little work to release it into a gas so it can be used to power a vehicle. For instance, water molecules contain two parts hydrogen & one part oxygen. Split the water molecules into their component parts & the result will be two parts hydrogen & one part oxygen.

The hydrogen engine uses fuel cells. These can be thought of as a cross between an internal combustion engine (petrol or diesel) & a battery. The hydrogen is stored in a pressurised tank & then fed into the fuel cell. It is not burnt; it is fused at the atomic level with oxygen from the environment to produce water. When this happens, electricity is released which is used to power an electric motor. The water that is made as a by-product in this process is so pure that if you should wish to, you could drink it. No pollutants are made in the process in any way whatsoever.

The fuel cell fuses the hydrogen & oxygen together in a process called an electrochemical reaction. It is a chemical reaction because it is a process which uses two chemical elements & it is also electric as this process produces electricity. This is why it is called an electrochemical reaction.

# Polymer exchange membrane fuel cell (PEM)

A fuel cell is split into three component parts, which is similar to a battery. It has a positively charged terminal, a negatively charged terminal & an electrolyte separating the two. The operation of the fuel cell follows the following steps.

Hydrogen gas from the tank is fed to the positive terminal whilst oxygen from the local environment is present at the negative terminal. The positive terminal is made from platinum & acts as a catalyst, because when the atoms of the hydrogen gas hit the catalyst, they split into hydrogen ions (protons) & electrons. The hydrogen ions are just the hydrogen atoms with their electrons removed.

The protons are positively charged, so are attracted to the negative terminal, so they are drawn through the electrolyte towards it. The electrolyte will only allow the protons to pass through it; therefore the electrons must pass through a bypass channel, where there just happens to be an electric motor. They therefore travel through the motor on their route to the negative terminal, thereby powering the motor on their way. The protons & the electrons then meet at the negative terminal & combine together with the oxygen molecules & as was seen earlier, two hydrogen molecules & one oxygen molecule makes water. This water is then released as either steam or water vapour.

The process will continue to function as long as hydrogen is fed to the positive terminal because there is an unlimited supply of oxygen within the atmosphere to complete the process. One fuel cell will produce approximately the same electricity as the output of an AA battery, therefore to power a vehicle multiple fuel cells are used & arranged in rows, then connected in a series to produce enough electricity to power the vehicle.

The second type of hydrogen engine utilises hydrogen in completely different manner.

# Hydrogen fuelled internal combustion engine

As was previously stated, hydrogen is not a fuel, but as has been seen in the petrol & diesel engine explanations, given the right environment it is possible to use many things as a fuel. Hydrogen does tick many boxes, after all it is a flammable gas, therefore much work has been undertaken in developing a hydrogen fuelled internal combustion engine & there are now several real world examples that are available to purchase, however there are many drawbacks to using hydrogen in this manner.

Firstly, even though hydrogen is a flammable gas, it is not as energy dense as other fuels, therefore a lot of hydrogen is needed to get any meaningful energy output when it is burnt. In addition to this, as well as a small amount water being produced as a result, the main exhaust gas that is produced is nitrogen oxide. This is the toxic emission gas that is currently causing so many problems for the motor industry; therefore it is not a clean burning engine & does not fall into what can be classed as a clean alternative.

Work is currently therefore being undertaken to develop a hydrogen/natural gas mix that will have emissions that are low enough to be classed as clean & pass the current emission regulations, but obtaining hydrogen from water is a very energy intensive process & therefore hydrogen is very expensive.
Reducing the hydrogen being burnt in the engine by increasing the air mixture does reduce the emissions, but this method reduces the resultant power output too. This reduces the power output to a feeble level as the hydrogen is not an energy dense gas to begin with.

The hydrogen fuelled internal combustion engine is therefore not an option for the foreseeable future, unless a method of obtaining a cheap supply of hydrogen is developed along with a method of making it cleanly, burning it cleanly & boosting the resultant energy output.

If using a PEM hydrogen vehicle appeals to you, it should be noted that currently there are only 14 filling stations in the whole of the UK that can supply hydrogen to vehicles. Unless this number greatly increases, or you plan making your own hydrogen, then life in a PEM will be somewhat prohibitive.

## How an electric engine works – in a nutshell

An electric engine is more commonly known as an electric motor. The electric motor receives its power from the controller & the controller gets the power from the batteries. It is in the batteries where the electric energy is chemically stored. When the electricity in the batteries is used up, it is replenished by either charging from a wall socket or from a charging unit. As it is not powered or charged by an internal combustion engine, these vehicles are considered to be 'all-electric' & usually known as battery electric vehicles (BEV's). The observant readers may have noticed some cars on the road that do not have an exhaust at the rear. These are BEV's & as they do not have an internal combustion engine, there is no need for an exhaust.

Batteries in general are very heavy. They therefore increase the overall weight of a BEV. As an example the Renault Zoe is a very small four seat BEV & it weighs 1943kg. The Ford fiesta which is a similar sized small four seat vehicle which uses an internal combustion engine weighs 1620kg. This extra weight can therefore pose problems for the designers because if the weight is placed too high up in the vehicle, it may become top heavy & then will run the risk of toppling over if corners are traversed at speed. To overcome this, the designers always place the batteries at a low level in the vehicles giving it a low centre of gravity, typically running them under the floor of the car or under the boot of the car. Using current technologies, a BEV will always weigh more than a vehicle using a petrol or diesel engine due to the weight of the batteries.

Despite having such a huge & heavy battery onboard a BEV, it still has an auxiliary battery like that found in a petrol or diesel engine vehicle because the auxiliary battery is used to power the lights, therefore even if the vehicles power pack batteries are empty, the lights will still work.

The controller (or control unit) is a small computer that decides how much of the electricity is moved from the batteries to the motor/s. If there was no controller, it would cause serious problems because the flow of electricity can either be switched on or off, just as with an electric light switch in your home. Therefore, the controller switches the supply on & off thousands of times every second & is therefore able to adjust exactly how much power is fed to the electric motor. The level of acceleration when the driver pushes the accelerator pedal is therefore interpreted by the controller & the level of electrical output is designed to mimic the feel of how an internal combustion engine would perform.

Electrical energy is then fed into the motor/s by the controller. Some BEV's have two motors, some have one. For example, the Nissan LEAF is front wheel drive & is powered from one motor. The Tesla Model S is rear wheel drive & is powered by one motor. There is also an all wheel drive Tesla Model S which is powered by two motors. The BMW i3 is rear wheel drive & has one motor, as does the Mitsubishi i-MiEV.

The optimal solution for the motors would be to have two on each axle. That way each wheel would be independently powered, there would be no need for gears, drive shafts, CV joints etc..

Each motor could even act as an e-brake, but there is a need for traditional brakes on the vehicle & the fact that each motor would need to be synchronised & be direct drive (un-geared), the complexity, added weight & costs would be prohibitive.

Therefore, one or two motors are currently used & they transfer power to the wheels via a prop shaft in the same manner as is found in a conventional petrol or diesel vehicle. Also, along with the prop shaft, there is the addition of a gear set that acts as a differential so that each of the two front wheels can rotate at different speeds, which allow the vehicle to turn left & right whilst stopping wheel slip. This is slightly different to a conventional gear box with different gear ratios which is found in traditional petrol or diesel vehicles as the electric motor is only coupled on a fixed gear ratio.

Charging the batteries can be undertaken in two ways. The first is when the brake pedal is pressed & this is called regenerative braking. In a typical vehicle braking system friction brakes are used. With friction brakes are used, when the brake pedal is pressed by the driver, the brakes function by grinding metal against metal which causes friction & this slows the speed of the vehicle. The energy is then dissipated through heat. However, with a regenerative braking system, the kinetic energy is transferred into electricity by using an electric motor which is utilised as an electric generator (any electric motor used in reverse acts as a generator). The electricity generated is then fed to the batteries.

This regenerative system can not act efficiently as a brake; therefore it must be used in tandem with friction brakes to ensure safe braking is achieved. This regenerative braking system is currently been used in F1 under the name 'kinetic energy recovery system' (KERS). Currently, only 20% of the kinetic energy produced during braking can be harvested & stored as electricity, therefore a more efficient method of battery charging in also used. That is by plugging the vehicle into the electrical grid with an electrical cable.

Plugging a vehicle into an electrical grid causes obvious problems. Firstly, the vehicle can not be used at all whilst it is being charged. This is a major problem as the primary function of any vehicle is to move from A to B, therefore for it to be immobile for hours a day is a massive drawback.

There is currently no universal standard for charging. Therefore there is AC electric (either single or three phase) & also DC electric charging. Each type (or family) of batteries requires a slightly different method of charging & the plugs used on different models differ from manufacturer to manufacturer. Therefore an attempt has been made to standardise things. Chapter 6 therefore covers the charging in greater detail.

Until a definitive charging standard is agreed, plugging an EV into a power point will need to be planned well in advance of any long journey. There are currently a small number of charging points in urban areas, but very few in rural locations. Recharging times are also a major consideration. Some vehicles can require 8 hours to fully charge & then may give a range of 80km. This may be fine for short trips perhaps back & forward to the shops or work, but on a long journey the charge time is a definite drawback. Some BEV's can be fast charged in 2 hours, but most of these will only allow one fast charge. It will need to then have at least one slow charge before it will accept another fast charge.

Most manufacturers do not publicise this, but hide this fact in the vehicle's user manual. Although the electric motors in a BEV work well enough to be practical, battery technology is not & therefore this is a major problem for any BEV. However, technology is always being developed & it should be expected that these drawbacks will reduce at some point in time when suitable enhancements are made to all the elements of the emerging BEV technologies.

Next, it is advantageous to look into each of the fuels that power these engines. In doing so, it will be possible to understand exactly what energy output level can be expected from each fuel; the anticipated level of pollution produced & therefore understand the financial & pollution costs per mile.

# Chapter 2 – **Fuels**

Each of the engines detailed in the previous chapter use fuel, but where do these fuels come from. Each of the fuels will therefore be examined to achieve a complete understanding of the impacts that these fuels have on your both your pocket & the environment. You may find the results somewhat surprising.

## **Fossil fuels**

Petrol does not start as a useable product. It comes from crude oil. It is crude oil that is pumped out of the ground & this is where the fossil fuels that are used in the world's vehicles are derived. The crude is sold by the barrel. That is 160 litres. The crude oil is then refined & separated (by a process called distillation[6]) into its residual components. On average, between 40 – 70 litres of petrol can be separated per barrel (but it is dependant on the actual make up of the crude oil, where it originated & the process used to refine it). OPEC have stated that 70 million barrels of oil are produced every day, which equates to almost 49,000 barrels every minute[7]. There are around 1,500 products that can be made from the crude oil in this way, but the most common are listed below (annual percentage from crude oil).

---

[6] https://en.wikipedia.org/wiki/Continuous_distillation#Continuous_distillation_of_crude_oil – 09/03/2019

[7] https://www.nationalgeographic.org/encyclopedia/petroleum/ - 10/03/2019

44.1% petrol (aka gasoline), 20.8% distillate fuel oil such as diesel oil & heating oil, 9.3% kerosene type fuel oil, 5.2% residual fuel oil, 4.3% liquefied refinery gasses, 4.3% still gas, 4.1% coke (the fuel), 2.9% asphalt & road oil, 2.7% petrochemical feedstock's, 1.1% lubricants, 0.5% kerosene & 0.7% other items.

The crude oil naturally forms underground, in reservoirs. When these are tapped to remove the contents, it is called a well. There is more pressure underground & also more heat than is found at the surface & as numerous other elements are dissolved in with the crude oil, when it is pumped to the surface, some of those dissolved elements can then begin to escape. For instance flammable gasses can escape from the crude oil as they are no longer confined at a high pressure. Hydrocarbons can also escape as solids. The exact chemical makeup of each of these underground reservoirs will vary from well to well. Some produce a high percentage of gasses (these are gas wells); some will produce a high proportion of crude oil (oil wells). Also, the exact molecular composition & proportion of crude oil & gasses will vary from well to well, but the chemical elements in crude oil will always fall within the following ranges.

83-85% carbon, 10-14% hydrogen, 0.1-2% nitrogen, 0.05-1.5% oxygen, 0.05-6.0% sulphur & <0.1% dissolved metals. The level of hydrocarbons contained within the crude oil also varies from well to well & they will always fall into the following ranges.

15-30% alkanes (paraffin), 30-60% cycloalkanes (naphthenes), 3-30% aromatics & the remainder being made from asphaltics.

The hydrocarbons are just carbon molecules with attached hydrogen molecules. In the crude oil these are found in chains of molecules, which are in the range of between 5-40 molecules in length. It is these chains that are used to make fuel. The chains of 1-4 molecules long form gasses, the chains being 5-8 molecules long are refined into petrol. Those being 9-16 molecules long are refined into diesel, kerosene & jet fuel. The ones over 16 are refined into fuel oil & lubricating oil. Whilst the chains of around 25 are made into paraffin wax. Asphalt is made from chains of molecules that are 35 & over.

These are all obtained by boiling the crude oil at various temperatures at a refinery with a process known as fractional distillation[8] because fractions are removed at varying temperatures. As the temperature increases, the products are removed, all at controllable & predictable temperatures.

Liquefied petroleum gas (LPG) is obtained from the crude oil at a temperature of -40°C. Butane is extracted between -12 to -1°C. Petrol is liberated in the range of -1 to 110°C, whilst jet fuel is produced at 150 -205°C. Kerosene is removed at 205 – 260°C & fuel oil between 205 to 290°C. Diesel is then taken out at in the temperature range between 260 to 315°C.

Petrol, diesel & flammable gasses & all the other petrochemical fuels are therefore refined from the crude oil by the same fractional distillation process. As the temperature rises, the crude oil releases its contents at the specified temperatures.

After being extracted from the crude oil, petrol is enhanced with certain additives to give some qualities that is desirable for use with the internal combustion engine. The first additive is used to increase the octane rating. That is the standard measure of performance for the engine fuel & expressed as a research octane number (RON).

---

[8] https://en.wikipedia.org/wiki/Fractional_distillation - 09/03/2019

The higher the octane number, the more compression the fuel can withstand before detonating (igniting). Fuels with a higher octane rating are used in high performance engines which require higher compression ratios. As was seen in the previous chapter, petrol engines operate with the ignition of air & fuel which is compressed together as a mixture. It is this mixture which is ignited at the end of the compression stroke using the spark plugs. Therefore, a high compression ratio of the fuel matters for petrol fuelled engines. If petrol with a low octane number is used, it may lead to the problem of engine knocking, which is when un-burnt portions of fuel is heated or compressed too much. Any un-burnt fuel can then self ignite before it should, or after the desired time & as a result cause damage to the engine.

In the UK, the petrol available at the forecourts usually are rated at 95 RON for unleaded petrol. Many also have what they call 'super' which has a 97 RON rating, but this is only suitable for performance engines. As a comparison, a small petrol powered two stroke outboard motor on a small boat would require a fuel with a 69 RON rating, with the highest rated freely available petrol having a 102 RON rating, but there are very few performance engines requiring a fuel of this level. In comparison, diesel oil has a rating somewhere between 15 – 25 RON. Within the EEC, 5% ethanol can also legally be added to the petrol. Ethanol has a 108.6 RON.

Liquefied petroleum gas (LPG) is a mixture of propane & butane, just propane or just butane. Propane has a 112 RON, whilst butane is 102 RON, therefore LPG is in the region of 102 – 112 RON, but it depends on the proportional mix of the gases.

Other additives are also placed into the petrol & these are designed to act as corrosion inhibitors, lubricants, metal deactivators, oxygenates & antioxidants. Typically, diesel fuels do not have a RON rating. Instead they have a cetane number. This is used as an indicator to the speed of combustion & also the compression needed for the ignition. The cetane number (CN) is important when determining the quality of the diesel fuel. The higher the CN, the shorter the delay before ignition. Within the EEC, the current minimum standard is 51 CN for regular diesel, whilst premium diesel fuel can have a CN as high as 60.

Biodiesel is generally in the range of 46 – 52 CN & animal fat based biodiesel often falls within the range of 56 – 60 CN, whilst waste vegetable oil (WVO) typically has a value of approximately 48 CN.

Petrol has a limited shelf life. In a sealed container it will store for approximately one year. If the seal is broken, it will have a shelf life of just six months at 20°C & only 3 months at 30°C. If it is left open to the elements, given time, the petrol will completely evaporate. Also, as petrol contains various components & each of these components degrade or evaporate at different rates, over time, the composition of the petrol will change significantly from its original design specification.

Diesel does not evaporate, but it will also store for one year within a sealed container. After this, it will start to turn to gum & the diesel will then tend to block filters in the engine. If diesel is left open to the elements it will degrade as it will act as a growing medium for fungus & bacteria which will degrade the diesel. Therefore treating stored diesel every six months will prolong its lifespan. Biodiesel has similar qualities to diesel & will degrade in the same way as diesel. LPG does not degrade when stored in a suitable container, nor does hydrogen.

# Hydrogen gas

As previously stated, hydrogen is the most abundant element in the universe & was the first element made after the big bang; however, it is no longer found floating about in its pure form because it quickly bonds to other elements to make other elements. Because of this, hydrogen atoms generally act as the foundation for other elements, bonding to them, building other elements just like tiny Lego bricks. Therefore the most abundant source of hydrogen in the world today is bound up in water. Each molecule of water is made up of two hydrogen atoms & one oxygen atom. Hydrogen atoms therefore need to be liberated from within other elements, typically from water. There is also a huge abundance of hydrogen locked up within hydrocarbons & even organic matter, but as there is so much water in the world, it is the easiest hydrogen containing element to source.

Hydrogen has the highest energy density in relation to mass of any other fuel or energy carrier. 1 kg of hydrogen contains as much energy as 2.1 kg of natural gas or even 2.8 kg petrol. In the USA, since the 1950's NASA has been the biggest user of hydrogen as they use hydrogen to fuel their liquid fuelled rockets when sending things up into space. The reason NASA uses hydrogen is because it packs more punch per weight than any other fuel.

Because the majority of the worlds hydrogen is locked inside other elements, it needs to be released before it can be used. There are currently two primary methods to achieve this (although there are several other methods). Electrolysis & steam-methane reforming (SMR).

The SMR method from natural gas (methane) is currently the cheapest method for obtaining hydrogen. 95% of hydrogen is produced using this method where, natural gas is heated to a temperate in the region of 700 - 1100°C & then combined with steam & a nickel catalyst.

This causes an endothermic reaction which breaks up the methane molecules & forms carbon monoxide & hydrogen gases. The carbon monoxide gas is then combined with more steam & channelled over iron oxide to undergo a water gas shift reaction with the aim of obtaining further quantities of hydrogen gas. Unfortunately, this process produces greenhouse gasses as a by product, therefore this method is not seen as a viable long term source for harvesting hydrogen. Honda has developed a Home Energy Station that performs SMR on a small scale & it is designed to fit within a typical domestic garage, but because natural gas is the feedstock, it releases carbon dioxide to the atmosphere which is a green house gas. Therefore this negates the whole point of using hydrogen as a replacement to petrol or diesel.

Alternatively, with the electrolysis method, electricity is passed through water & this liberates the hydrogen atoms from the oxygen atoms. It is this same method which is employed on submarines to produce oxygen. Electrolysis is the simplest method & has proven to be in the region of 70 – 80% efficient. 1.23v of DC electricity is all that is needed to split the water molecules, which is not a huge amount of power. In fact it is possible to use a small AA battery to do this, but it takes as much energy to take apart a water molecule as can be achieved from the hydrogen, therefore it is not an ideal scenario because it takes the same level of energy to power the process as can be realised from the hydrogen that is produced.

In fact, the cost of producing electricity (even using wind turbines & solar PV) is far more expensive than the cost of natural gas. It is therefore not a financially viable method for obtaining hydrogen.

However, it is possible to harvest your own hydrogen at home using a solar panel &/or wind turbine linked to an electrolyser. The electrolyser is the equipment that is needed to undertake the electrolysis, which was explained earlier, where water is split into its individual atoms, just by passing electricity through it. The electrolyser is similar to a battery, but works in reverse.

Batteries operate by having chemicals packed within a sealed container that have two electrical terminals dipping into them. When the terminals are connected to a circuit, the chemicals undergo reactions inside the container & produce electricity which then in turn flows through the circuit. An electrolyser works when two terminals are placed in a container. These terminals are then connected to a battery of power source & then electricity is passed through the solution (water in this case). A chemical reaction will then take place & the water is split into its constituent atoms. Hydrogen gas will form at the negative electrode, whilst oxygen gas will collect at the positive electrode. It is then just a matter of collecting & storing the hydrogen gas for future use. These electrolysers can cost in the region of £100 up to several thousand pounds. Obviously, the higher the cost, the higher the output, but bottling & storage of the hydrogen gas could prove to be an even more expensive & difficult exercise.

Regarding energy, as previously stated, by weight, 1kg of hydrogen contains 33.33kWh of useable energy. Petrol contains 12kWh, but by volume, hydrogen does not perform quite so well. Petrol has 8.8kWh per litre, diesel has 10kWh per litre & hydrogen has 0.003kWh per litre. This is due to the fact that at room temperature & pressure, hydrogen's density is so low that it contains less than one-three-hundredth the energy than the equivalent volume of petrol. Therefore, a greater amount of hydrogen would be required to drive the same distance as a typical petrol or diesel vehicle, even though the graph in chapter 1 shows that hydrogen is very energy dense. It therefore needs to be compressed to a high degree to achieve this level of output.

In addition, hydrogen can make steel & other metals very brittle, weakening them to the point of fracture. Taking into account all these facts, the initial expense in obtaining hydrogen & the difficulties involved with storing it; it quickly becomes a very expensive & dangerous fuel.

# Electricity

Electricity is not a fuel that can be mined or obtained naturally. It is caused when the electrons that surround an atom's nucleus are stimulated. These electrons are made of energy; therefore any agitation applied to them causes their energy to disperse. Metal atoms happen to be good conductors because their nucleuses have a loose hold on their outlying electrons, making these electrons easier to stimulate. Materials such as glass & ceramics have nucleuses that have a firm hold over their electrons; therefore these materials are very poor conductors of electricity.

For electricity to flow, a current has to be made & subsequently maintained. This is achieved by using a generator. Generators are what keep the electrons stimulated & moving. The process of generating energy, in effect, creates more. Once a current of electricity is conducted, a device called a transformer directs the flow so that it can be put to some form of use. An electric current runs efficiently along copper wiring. The generator then acts as a magnetic force that stimulates the electron currents to run along the wiring. This is how electricity is made.

In practical terms, turbines are attached to electricity generators. These can be described basically as tight coils of copper wound around an iron core which is free to rotate inside a magnet. As the inner part turns, the magnetism is converted into electricity; therefore the magnetic force is transformed into electricity.
This electricity then travels out of the generator to where the electricity is to be used or where it can be stored in batteries for future use. Unfortunately turbines are usually made to spin by steam that has been made by burning fossil fuels such as oil, coal or gas, or even by using nuclear power. All of these fossil fuels & nuclear power are used to boil water to produce steam that is then fed through the turbines to create electricity in attached generators. Hydro electricity is different; it is when gravity fed water is channelled through a turbine.

The International Energy Agency (IEA) reports that in 2016, the worlds electricity production was as follows: 38.4% produced by burning coal, 23.2% produced by burning natural gas, 16.3% from hydro, 10.4% from nuclear fission, 3.7% from burning oil & 8% from renewables that are not hydro.

Therefore in 2016 65.3% of all electricity in the world was obtained by burning fossil fuels. Every country has different resources, so each country has different sources for their electrical generation. France uses a high proportion of nuclear fission, therefore only 10% of its electricity is produced from burning fossil fuels. However in the USA, 70% of the electricity is generated from fossil fuels, whilst in China 80% of their electricity is made from burning fossil fuels.

As most energy scientists agree, burning fossil fuels contribute to the greenhouse effect, but it is down to each & every power plant just how polluting their emissions are. Some are better than others, but there are no zero emission power plants. Therefore why is it claimed that electricity is a clean fuel? It is actually acknowledged that electricity is clean only at the point of use, not at source. By using electricity in a car that is hailed as being a zero emission vehicle does not make it a non polluting vehicle as the electricity was generated at a polluting power station. The emissions were just made elsewhere, not at the vehicle. This therefore displaces the pollution; it does not remove it from the world.

Perhaps, electricity made from renewable energy sources will fare better. After all, wind turbines & solar electricity has been hailed as being the future for mankind as a sustainable way to produce electricity. Again, they both just displace the pollution, they do not remove it. As an example, the large wind turbines favoured by electricity companies are principally made from steel & also copper wires. In 2017 49.2% of the worlds steel originated in China. Chile is the world's largest supplier of copper with China being the second biggest supplier.

Therefore statistically, a high proportion of the materials used in the construction of these windmills were mined, processed, refined & produced on the opposite side of the world before being transported to Europe, the USA, or wherever they were destined to be used. Every step of the way fossil fuels were burnt. Just because the windmill does not pollute the environment when it is operational, does not mean its production or transportation did not pollute the environment. The same is true with solar panels as 60% of them are made in China. Most western governments & organisations conveniently ignore these simple facts as they have targets set by umbrella organisations operating under the United Nations to which they have agreed to operate under. Western countries claim they are reducing pollution, & then point their finger at the countries that have made their 'green energy products' for not doing enough to reduce pollution. It is pure hypocrisy.

This is not the only 'issue' with electricity in the developed world as every home has electrical appliances that all use electricity; therefore every household faces a sizeable annual bill for their energy use. No doubt, most households have washing machines, fridge freezers, televisions, radios, computers, phones, DVD players, satellite receivers, hi-fi's, microwave ovens, alarm clocks, lighting, heating. The list goes on & on. Yet, using each & every one of these appliances costs money to run & this cost is set to rise year on year as fossil fuels are slowly depleted & demand for electricity rises.

Whilst demand for fossil fuels increases, so too will the cost. It is a simple case of demand outstripping supply which causes this monetary rise in costs.

In the UK, the 'National Grid' predicts the cost of electricity to double by 2035 & gas to rise by 33% over the same time period. This is due to various factors, depletion of fossil fuels, governmental 'green energy incentives', lack of investment & most telling, the fact that by 2035, the UK is predicted to need to import 90% of its energy needs[9]. In addition, the US Energy Information Administration (EIA) also predicts an increase of 48% in total world energy demand by 2040[10].

The cost of obtaining energy has risen 20% since 2009 & will clearly continue to increase. In addition, the likelihood of power cuts will also increase dramatically in the near future. The UK's Big Infrastructure Group (BIG) has warned that in the UK, the spare capacity of electrical energy that was ready to be delivered to consumers has fallen sharply in recent years. In 2011 - 2012 it was 17%, whilst in 2016 - 2017 it had fallen to just 1% thereby increasing the likelihood of blackouts. BIG are not alone in predicting blackouts in the UK, the Institute of Mechanical Engineers predict that the UK will only have half the energy it needs by 2025 & they have also stated that "The UK is facing an electricity supply crisis"[12].

Despite these predictions, both the UK & the EEC have announced that they intend to legislate to outlaw the sale of all new diesel & petrol vehicles by 2040[13].

---

[9] https://www.theguardian.com/environment/2014/jul/10/price-electricity-double-next-20-years-national-grid - 28/08/2017

[10] https://www.eia.gov/todayinenergy/detail.php?id=26212 – 28/08/2017

[12] https://theenergyst.com/uk-facing-power-blackouts-engineers-warn/ - 28/08/2017

[13] https://www.ft.com/content/7e61d3ae-718e-11e7-93ff-99f383b09ff9 - 09/09/2017

The Green Alliance has stated that the UK grid is not ready for the anticipated demand that electric vehicles will place on the grid & that blackouts will occur as a result because it takes the same amount of electricity that an average household uses in three days to charge one electric car overnight[14]. They add that by 2025, 700,000 UK consumers will be experiencing blackouts due to this level of demand & also because of the damage caused by the increased level of strain on the UK network. The UK electricity network was never designed to cope with these rising levels of load.

Therefore in summary, electricity is not a clean zero emission fuel as the UK, along with most of the developed world rely on fossil fuels to generate it. The developed countries in the world do not have the infrastructure to cope with the predicted levels of the increased demand when electric vehicles become common place & the basic cost of electricity will increase, whilst delivery will at best become sporadic. At the same time, it will become more difficult to source petrol or diesel vehicles, or even the fuels to run them. It may therefore be prudent to invest in your own electrical energy production facility using wind &/or solar power, just to ensure that you can drive your vehicle & keep the lights on at home. It may even turn out to be the only option for obtaining affordable electricity.

Therefore, the author recommends the following books by P Xavier if you wish to future proof your energy needs:

- DIY home energy solutions.
- Everything you ever wanted to know about wind turbines for domestic power, but were afraid to ask.
- Everything you ever wanted to know about solar panels for domestic power, but were afraid to ask.
- Everything you ever wanted to know about batteries for domestic power, but were afraid to ask.

---

[14] https://www.theguardian.com/business/2017/apr/20/uk-unprepared-for-surge-in-electric-car-use-thinktank-warns - 09/09/2017

# Chapter 3 – **Electric cars need batteries**

There are currently numerous makes & models of electric cars available on the market today & each one is different. However, they all have one thing in common & that is they all have batteries to power their motors.

## Batteries

Everyone knows what a battery is, or at least what it is used for. It is a storage facility for electricity & every car has a battery. When any battery is supplying electricity, the positive terminal is known as the cathode & the negative terminal is known as the anode. The negative terminal is the source of electrons that will flow through an external electric circuit to the positive terminal.

Petrol & diesel cars have what is known as a starting, lighting & ignition (SLI) battery, which is designed to deliver a huge amount of electricity over a very short period, which is when the vehicle is started. When the engine is running, the alternator provides the electrical power & also recharges the SLI battery. These SLI batteries are therefore beyond the scope of this book & as such, the batteries covered here are solely those used in electric vehicles.

Electric vehicles use a different type of battery as they do not need a huge electrical surge when starting, but instead, deliver their electrical energy over a sustained period of time. These are often referred to as deep cycle batteries. They will therefore be abbreviated in this book as electric vehicle batteries (EVB's). All the EVB's covered in this chapter fall into the deep cycle battery family.

When compared to petrol or diesel, any battery will have a very low energy density. That can be basically explained by comparing it to another fuel. A battery weighing 1kg has a lot less energy than 1kg of petrol. Therefore, numerous batteries would be needed to power a vehicle to attain the same distance that a comparable petrol vehicle would achieve on 1kg of fuel. Much work has therefore been undertaken to find smaller, lighter batteries that have a higher power to weight ratio. Despite all this work, batteries still do not compare with a petrol or diesel fuels with regard to a source of power.

The EVB's that are currently used in electric vehicles are all rechargeable & are based on the following chemistries. Lead–acid (flooded, deep-cycle & VRLA), NiCd, nickel–metal hydride, lithium-ion, Li-Ion polymer. Zinc–air & molten-salt batteries are also used, but are not so common. The most common type is lithium-ion & lithium polymer due to their higher energy density compared to other batteries. Each of these battery types will now be examined individually.

## Lead-Acid

These are the most common battery within the deep-cycle battery market, they are also the cheapest & this technology has been around for approximately 100 years. They will therefore still be available for the foreseeable future due to their established manufacturing base which currently exists around the globe.

If a lead-acid battery is properly maintained, then it should function within the range of 80 – 90% efficiency. Wherever possible a full charge should be made when not driving the vehicle because this will maintain the batteries life & it will therefore retain its efficiency. They can however become damaged if they are overcharged or over-discharged.

A variant that has a lower requirement for battery maintenance is called a valve regulated lead-acid (VRLA) battery. Another variant that needs regular maintenance (perhaps once a month or so) is called flooded lead-acid. These are approximately half the cost of VRLA batteries.

Of the sealed types, there are two. Gel & absorbed gas mat (AGM). They are not fully sealed as they have a valve fitted that allows for any off-gassing that may occur, as such any battery store MUST be well ventilated. Gel batteries are designed to be recharged at a slower rate; as such they are not really suitable for the EVB market. The AGM batteries are therefore the best type as they are better suited to the recharge phase. Also, AGM batteries are cheaper & lighter than gel.

All lead-acid batteries have large capacities compared to their counterparts but the flooded types are less common. They do however offer the lowest cost per kWh, so you definitely get more bang to your buck.

Flooded batteries also retail at about half the cost of VRLA, offer a slightly better energy/capacity ratio & are available in larger capacities. The chances of failure are greater with flooded batteries if they are not properly maintained. They must be well ventilated & could cause a hazard if their internal liquid spills.

The problem with all these lead acid batteries is that they should never be discharged below 50% of their capacity, as it shortens the battery's life. They therefore do not lend themselves to the EVB market; however they have been successfully used for many years in golf carts, forklift trucks & milk floats. Deep-cycle lead-acid batteries do tend to be expensive & have a much shorter life span than the vehicle itself. They may need to be replaced every 3 years or so, but because they use an old & widespread technology, their recycling rates can be as high as 95% in some countries.

## Zinc-air fuel cells

These are mechanically rechargeable batteries. That is when a component needs to be physically replaced after it has decayed & then the need arises to charge the unit. They are metal–air batteries that receive their charge by oxidizing zinc with oxygen from the air. These batteries have very high energy densities & are relatively inexpensive to produce.
The charging method is not achieved by plugging the unit into a power source; instead the anode & electrolyte need to be physically replaced. Alternatively the charge can be achieved by adding zinc powder to restart the chemical reaction. These types of batteries were investigated by various militaries in the 1960's, but were dropped in favour of lithium batteries which offer higher discharge rates & easier handling. Since then, zinc-air batteries have been investigated for use as EVB's, where a zinc electrolyte paste or pellets are placed into a chamber in the battery & the waste zinc oxide is pumped into a waste tank. Fresh zinc paste or pellets are added to a fuel tank & the waste zinc oxide is pumped out at a fuel station to be recycled.

The reason why these batteries have been considered as EVB's is that there is 100 times more zinc in the world than lithium & the world's production of zinc will be enough to power one billion vehicles. Current production levels of lithium will only power ten million lithium-ion vehicles. Busses using this technology have been successfully used in Singapore to power busses, but it no car manufacturer has as yet designed a car around this battery technology.

## Sodium–nickel chloride (Zebra)

There is a variant of a molten salt battery (sometimes called a hot salt battery) developed in 1985 by 'zeolite battery research Africa', hence the name Zebra battery that is suitable for use as an EVB.

The zebra battery operates at 245°C & uses molten sodium tetrachloroaluminate NaAlCl$_4$ (which has a melting point of 157°C) as the electrolyte. The positive electrode is nickel; when the battery is in its discharged state & then nickel chloride when in its charged state. The negative electrode is molten sodium.

These Zebra batteries are currently used in several electric vans & the US Postal Service are currently undergoing field tests with the aim of utilising this chemistry in their electric delivery vans.

Due to the high operating temperature for zebra batteries, their downside is that when not in use, they need to be kept heated, as if the internal chemicals are left to cool & solidify, they will need approximately 12 hours to re-heat & recharge before they can be re-used, therefore these batteries may be suitable for some vehicle applications, but not for general unpredictable motoring that is experienced with most domestic car use.

## Nickel Cadmium (NiCd or NiCad)

These are typically very rugged batteries & use nickel oxide hydroxide & metallic cadmium as electrodes. They are cheap to make & therefore can also be bought cheaply. They tend to have an efficiency range of between 70 – 90% & have the benefit of being quick to charge & will tolerate abuse very well. Maintenance will however extend their lifespan even further. These also function well in low temperatures compared to many newer batteries. Unfortunately, these NiCd batteries have a very low energy density. Their biggest drawback is the fact that they are not recyclable & contain toxic metals. They also suffer from memory problems when they are repeatedly charged. It is already very difficult to dispose of them due to their toxic makeup & as time goes on it may well prove to be impossible. They are therefore now becoming quite hard to source as they are being phased out in favour of nickel-metal-hydride (NiMH).

## Nickel-Metal-Hydride (NiMH)

These are similar to NiCd batteries as both use nickel oxide hydroxide (NiOOH). However, the negative electrodes use a hydrogen-absorbing alloy instead of cadmium. A NiMH battery can have between two or three times the capacity of an equivalent size NiCd battery & its energy density can be near to that of a lithium-ion battery. A NiMH can also have an efficiency range of between 66 – 92% & also have the benefit of being fast to charge. They have an excellent energy density, but if they are repeatedly deep cycled, their performance will deteriorate after approximately 200 cycles (200 days use) because they prefer shallow cycling. They take a longer time to charge than NiCd & produce heat whilst being charged. They also do not perform very well in higher temperatures & therefore need to be stored at lower temperatures. They also require to be regularly discharged to prevent crystals forming within the battery. They are currently 20% more expensive than NiCD.

## Lithium-Ion (Li-Ion)

Developments in battery technologies have led to Li-Ion batteries. These developments have now reached a level that Li-Ion have become a serious alternative to lead-acid batteries. They are now the obvious choice in the EVB market so are now being continually researched by the automotive industry to further increase their efficiency. At present they have an efficiency range of between 80 – 90%.

However, lithium is a highly reactive alkali metal element, but is also one of the lightest. It would float on water if it didn't react violently to it. It bursts into flames upon any contact with water. It also reacts violently in normal atmospheric conditions because of its spontaneous reaction with oxygen. Li-Ion batteries therefore contain a highly volatile element which could cause problems if they were ever to malfunction.

They do however have a higher cell voltage & therefore one Li-Ion battery would be equivalent to three NiCd or NiMH batteries. They also do not contain a liquid electrolyte, therefore they do not leak. They are 4 times more energy dense than any lead-acid battery, so less batteries are required in a vehicle. They can retain their charge for up to 10 years & do not suffer from any memory effect. They are designed to have a long lifecycle (3000 charge – discharges), whilst lead-acid have a lower lifecycle (typically max. 500), therefore the Li-Ion technology appear ideal for use in an electric vehicle.

They do however have the potential to be very dangerous (if not manufactured correctly they can spontaneously catch fire – there have been many recalls due to these batteries, most famously the Samsung Galaxy Note 7), they are also more expensive than lead-acid batteries.

They can also be discharged (Depth of Discharge – DOD) 100%, whilst lead-acid batteries can only be discharged to a maximum of 80% & most lead-acid manufacturers do not recommend discharging lead-acid by more than (DOD) 50%. There are also many variants to this battery, some of which are: Lithium-ion polymer, lithium cobalt ($LiCoO_2$), lithium manganese ($LiMn_2O_4$), lithium nickel ($LiNiO_2$), lithium nickel cobalt manganese $Li(NiCoMn)O_2$, lithium nickel cobalt aluminium $Li(NiCoAl)O_2$, lithium iron phosphate ($LiFePO_4$), lithium metal polymer, lithium sulphur ($Li_2S_8$) & one called 'alternative anode chemistry' (LTO), & these are just a few of the variants being developed, each of which has different properties & are therefore being developed for a wide range of applications.

The three most common are: iron phosphate ($LiFePO_4$) as it is relatively safe & has a long design life, lithium nickel cobalt manganese $Li(NiCoMn)O_2$ due to its high energy to weight ratio & lithium nickel cobalt aluminium $Li(NiCoAl)O_2$ which is ideal in electric vehicles as it has the highest energy to weight ratio.

Lithium-Ion batteries do gradually degrade at the end of their life which is far better than the sudden death which lead-acid batteries are prone to experience. Lithium-ion batteries also contain less toxic metals than any lead-acid battery & are therefore lithium-ion batteries are categorised as non-toxic waste. They can therefore be safely incinerated & even recycled safely.

Finally, all lithium-ion batteries are fitted with an internal 'battery management system' (BMS) to control the individual battery & stop any over heating during their charging period, which can therefore reduce the overall weight of the electrics in an electric vehicle, protect the battery & enhance its lifespan.

All batteries have problems coping with hot & cold temperatures because the temperature will affect the power output. However, Li-Ion batteries do tend to outperform other battery chemistries at high both high & low temperatures. EVB's therefore have their own heating & cooling systems. At high & low temperatures, Li-Ion batteries will slow the rate of charge to avoid any potential damage occurring & in very cold temperatures, even the Li-Ion batteries can loose up to 25% (DOD) of their charge, seriously reducing their range.

## A refresher on electricity

There are some terms that you need to be familiar with before being able to understand exactly how much electricity a battery can hold.

**Voltage** is the measure of electrical potential. It is measured in volts (V). This can be thought of as pressure. If you think of water travelling through a pipe, the greater the pressure pushing the water through that pipe, the greater the volume of water will travel through that pipe every minute.

If you now envisage an electric supply charging a battery, then the electricity will 'flow' to the battery. The greater the voltage being fed to the battery, the more electricity will flow into the battery.

If there is no voltage, then there is no current. There is no 'flow'. Nothing is moving. Power is only present when voltage & current are present.

**Current** (or amperage) is the measure of the flow of electricity. This is expressed as amperes or amps (A). This can be thought of as how fast something is moving; imagine a car travelling at 60mph on a motorway, then similarly electricity is travelling from the electric supply, through a cable to a battery at 60 amps. The speed at which electricity travels is actually very fast, much quicker than a car can travel. One amp is the equivalent to 6 billion, billion ($6.2415 \times 10^{18}$) electrons per second. Therefore 60 amps is extremely fast.

Electrical **resistance** is the value given for how much a conductor opposes the flow. It is expressed in Ohms ($\Omega$). It is the relationship of voltage & current, therefore if low resistance is desired then you need a high voltage, not high current. This is basically opting for a big pipe to allow a large flow of water through rather than pushing water very fast through a small straw. The small straw would offer resistance & therefore seem to fight back.

A batteries power **capacity** is how much electrical energy is stored within in. A Watt is equivalent to 1 joule of energy & it is expressed as Watt-hours. For example a 20w light bulb will require 20 watts (20 joules of energy) to function for an hour. A battery to power it will therefore need to supply 20Wh.
One thousand watts is 1 kilo watt, therefore a 2 kWh battery will supply 2,000 watts of electricity per hour, enough to supply 100 20w light bulbs for an hour. The power rating for EVB's tend to be expressed in kWh.

As an example, the Mitsubishi i MiEV has a lithium-ion battery pack that provides 16kWh which allows this EV to achieve a top speed of 130km/h (81 mph) & a theoretical range of 170km (106 miles). This Mitsubishi is also badged within Europe as a Citroën C-Zero & Peugeot iOn. Whilst the Nissan LEAF II has a 30kWh lithium-ion battery giving a top speed of 150 km/h (93 mph) & a theoretical range of 172km (107 miles).

The EVB is only a part of the EV picture as the battery is just used to power the motor which turns the wheels.

## Battery charging

All EVB's will need to be charged or they will rapidly be depleted. They will also need charging more frequently & for much longer than the refuelling of any petrol or diesel vehicle. This is due to the fact that an EVB will only hold a small percentage of the equivalent energy that a tank of petrol or diesel will hold. Confusingly, there are several methods of charging an EVB. The first is achieved by plugging the car into either a domestic electrical socket, or by plugging the car into a purpose made & specific charging point.

There are numerous cabling & plug options too, so these are all covered in detail in chapter 6, therefore the only charging option to be covered here will be onboard charging.

## Regenerative braking, e-braking or KERS

Regenerative braking (aka e-braking or KERS) is a method of recovering energy when slowing a vehicle or object by converting the kinetic energy into electricity to be used either immediately or stored in the battery. The electric motor uses the vehicle's momentum to recover energy that would be otherwise be dissipated & subsequently lost through friction at the brake discs, where it is lost as heat. Regenerative braking has the benefit of improving the overall efficiency of the brakes as regeneration will greatly extend the life span of the braking system as well as providing an 'on the go' charge to the battery.

This method of charging is possible as the electric motor can also be used as an electric generator when the brake pedal is pressed (which is covered in the next chapter). Modern hybrids & EV's use regenerative braking as a method of charging solely to extend the range of their vehicles.

Manufacturers typically only offer figures regarding the theoretical range of their vehicles from cable based charging as this is easier to calculate accurately & is generally easier for the driver to understand.

## EVB's used in BEV's

As was stated previously, the batteries in a BEV are different to those found in an ICE powered vehicle & they are far bigger. Bigger in size, but also with regard to the amount of electrical energy they can hold & deliver. Each BEV has a different specification; therefore here the Tesla Model S will be examined.

The battery used in a Tesla Model S is a 85kWh lithium ion.

*Figure 2 Tesla Model S 85kWh battery pack (Public Domain Image 2019)*

However, this battery is made up from many smaller batteries & together they add up to the desired level of output (85kWh). This is exactly the same method that is employed in a small torch. For instance, one that uses two AA batteries is a 3v torch as each of the two AA batteries delivers 1.5v. In the Tesla Model S, it would take thousands of AA batteries to deliver the 85kWh & that is exactly what it does. It uses many small batteries (which look like AA batteries), that are connected together so that they can deliver the required level of electrical power.

The batteries that Tesla use in their Model S are called 18650 cells because they measure 18mm x 65mm. 7,104 of these cells (subdivided into 16 modules with each module containing 6 groups of 74 cells are connected in parallel & each of the 6 groups are wired in series) are packed together into a large battery pack weighing 540 kg (1,200 lb).

The picture on the previous page shows how the entire battery pack from the Model S is constructed, with just the top cover removed to view the internal contents. The following diagram is a closer view of an individual module & a close up view of where the tops of a small number of the 18650 batteries are visible.

Each of these battery cells are connected to give the desired level of output. As was mentioned earlier, each of the 74 cells are connected together in a parallel arrangement (called a group), then each of these groups are connected together in a series arrangement.

*Figure 3 Close up of the Tesla Model S battery (Public Domain Image 2019)*

The reason why the batteries are connected in this fashion is because a series connection will have a different output result than a parallel connection. They are therefore grouped in this fashion to provide the exact output level that is required to power the electric motor.

## Series or parallel

To connect batteries together in a series, the positive terminal needs to be connected to the negative terminal on the next battery. By adopting a series connection, the voltage will double but the amperage will remain the same.

## Series connection

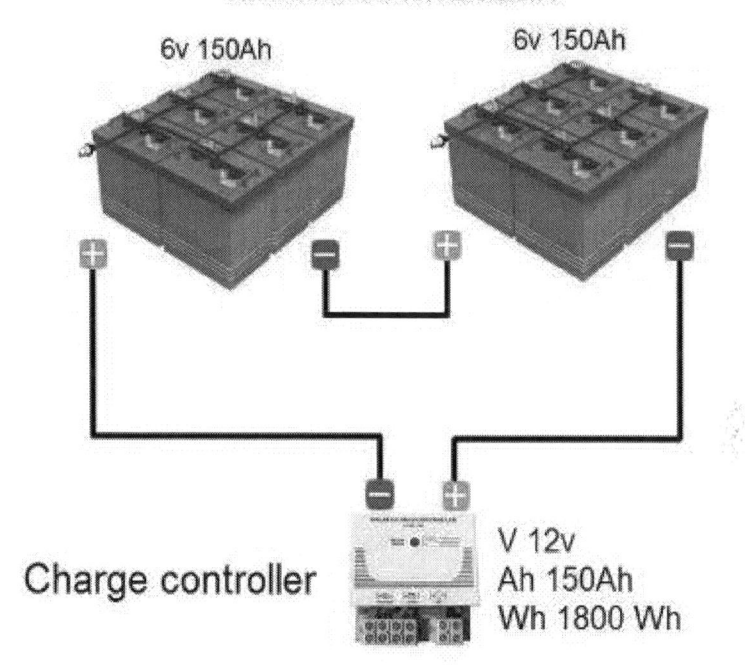

*Figure 4 Batteries connected with a series connection (P Xavier 2017)*

Figure 4 shows that by connecting two 6v 150Ah batteries together using a series connection will double the voltage to 12v, but the amperage will remain as 150Ah.

Conversely, if batteries are connected together with a parallel connection (all the positive terminals together & all negative terminals together) the amperage will double but the voltage will remain the same.

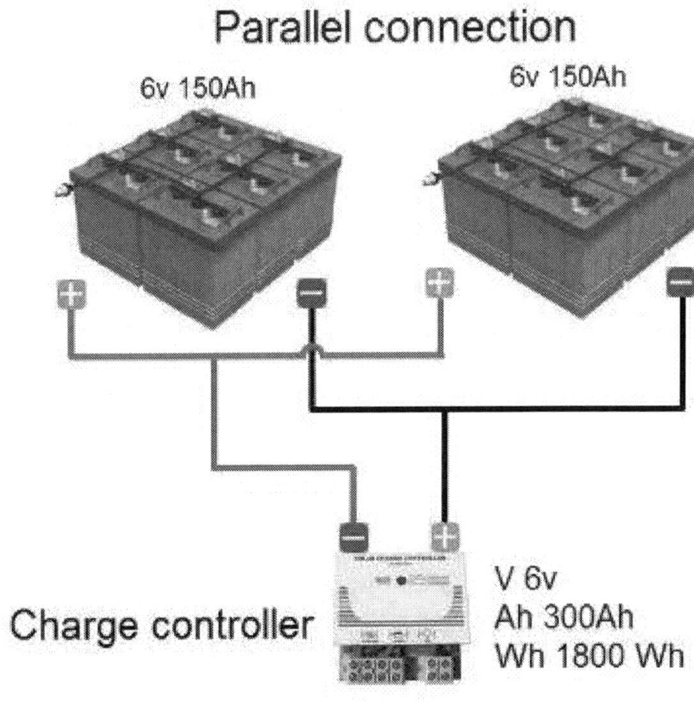

## Parallel connection

6v 150Ah     6v 150Ah

Charge controller

V 6v
Ah 300Ah
Wh 1800 Wh

*Figure 5 Batteries connected with a parallel connection (P Xavier 2017)*

Figure 5 shows that by connecting the same two 6v 150Ah batteries together using a parallel connection, the voltage will remain as 6v, but now the amperage will double to 300Ah. Therefore the combination of connecting the batteries into groups allows the desired output to be achieved, which in the case of the Tesla Model S is 85kWh. As a comparison, the Nissan LEAF uses a 24kWh lithium ion manganese oxide battery, constructed from 192 cells which are arranged into 48 modules of 4 cells to give the resultant 24kWh.

18650 batteries are not the only batteries that are used in EV's. There is also the type used in mobile phones. This is called a prismatic cell & does not have a cylinder shape like an AA battery, but is generally shaped like a very small paperback book.

That is an oblong block. They are available in small sizes that are suitable for mobile phones & also large sizes suitable for larger applications such as the large cells that can deliver capacities of 20–50Ah. BMW use a 42.2kWh lithium manganese prismatic cell battery in their i3.

Another battery type is the pouch battery, which looks very much like a pouch of freeze dried food. The pouch allows the internal chemistry of the battery to expand & contract without damaging the outer layers which can cause a failure. The Chevrolet Bolt (badged as a Opel Ampera-e in Europe) uses a 60kWh lithium ion pouch battery made from 288 individual pouch cells which are bundled into groups of three that are connected in parallel. The 96 groups of three are connected in a series connection to make up the entire 60kWh battery.
As these batteries are used to power the electric motors in the EV's, it would now be prudent to examine these motors in detail.

# Chapter 4 – **Electric cars need electric motors**

Every make & model of electric cars (even hybrids) available today uses an electric motor instead of or with an internal combustion engine (ICE), but there are variants. There is not one standard motor. Therefore, it would be beneficial to examine how they are used & what types are used.

## Electric motors

In simplistic terms, an electric motor has already been described in this book. In the chapter on fuels under the sub heading of electricity, where an electricity generator powered by a steam turbine was briefly described, where the movement of the turbine (rotating) generated electricity within the generator. The inner moving part generated electricity in the outer part. The electric motor works in exactly the same way, but in reverse. Electricity in the outer part generates movement on the inner part (rotating). This is why these motors can also be used to charge the batteries when they are used for regenerative braking (KERS) as these motors can also be used as a generator. There is a bit more to an electric motor than that, but in basic terms, that is how they work.

To give a little bit more detail, electrical energy is supplied to the stator from the battery. The coils within the stator (made from the conducting wire) are arranged on opposite sides of the stator core & act as electromagnet. Therefore, when the electrical energy from the car battery is supplied to the motor, these coils create a rotating magnetic field that turns the rotor. The spinning rotor is what creates the mechanical energy that is needed to rotate the gears, which in turn, powers the wheels.

With a car powered by an ICE, there is an alternator which is powered by the battery. This gives power to start the engine, which powers the gears & then turns the wheels. The engine when running, then powers the alternator in the ICE car & it is the alternator that recharges the battery.

In an EV, there is no alternator. It is the electric motor in the EV that acts as both motor & also as an alternator. In an ICE vehicle, the battery starts the motor, which rotates the gears, which in turn, spins the wheels. But when you press the accelerator pedal in an EV; the rotor gets turned by the rotating magnetic field providing the torque. However, when pressure is removed from the accelerator pedal, the rotating magnetic field in the electric motor stops & the rotor starts spinning faster (as it is not being pulled along by the magnetic field, momentum then takes over) as there is no load on the motor. It is now spinning faster than it did with the rotating magnetic field. This action then recharges the battery, so the motor is now acting as an alternator. It will continue to do this until the accelerator pedal is pressed once more. Early EV's used direct current (DC) electric motors, but newer EV's are now typically fitted with alternating current (AC) electric motors. AC & DC will be explored in the following chapter, as here just the motor components will be examined in greater detail.

## Motor parts

All electric motors follow the same principles & therefore have many of the same components. Electricity flows around the outer part & this causes the inner part to spin. This spin (torque) is then transferred to the wheels either directly through each axle or via the driveshaft as was described earlier in chapter 1.

The **armature** or **rotor** is the centre part (the part that spins) is a cylinder that either contains conductors to carry electrical currents, or carry permanent magnets. The conductors interact with the magnets to generate the motion.

The rotor is supported within the motor by **bearings**. This does nothing more than hold the rotor in place & allow it to spin freely.

Placed around the rotor (but not touching it) is the **stator** & this is either made up of windings or permanent magnets. The inner most part of the stator is usually made from numerous thin metal sheets. These are called laminations. These laminations are used to reduce energy losses that would result if a solid core were used. The stator does not touch the rotor & the rotor is allowed to turn freely & unhindered within the motor. This space between them is called the air gap.
This **air gap** is as small as possible because a large gap will have a very big negative effect on the performance of the motor as the magnetising current increases with the distance within the air gap. Therefore, the air gap should be as small as possible. However there is a slight trade off as very small gaps could cause mechanical problems, create noise & cause friction wear.

The wires that are wound around the outside in coils are called **windings**. These windings are wrapped around a laminated iron magnetic core to form magnetic poles when they are energised with an electric current. These are found in one of two basic magnet field pole configurations, salient & non-salient pole configurations.

The salient pole configuration is when the poles magnetic field is produced by a winding wound around the pole below the pole face. The non-salient pole configuration, or round-rotor machine, the winding is distributed in pole face slots.

The final part is the **commutator**. This operates as a switch in DC motors & some AC motors. Because with DC motors, the rotor will only spin through 180° before stopping, the commutator acts as a switch, changing the polarity of the magnetic field, allowing the rotor to continue to spin through a further 180° before switching again & again. Most AC motors do not use a commutator as the current reverses periodically & therefore there is no need for such a switch.

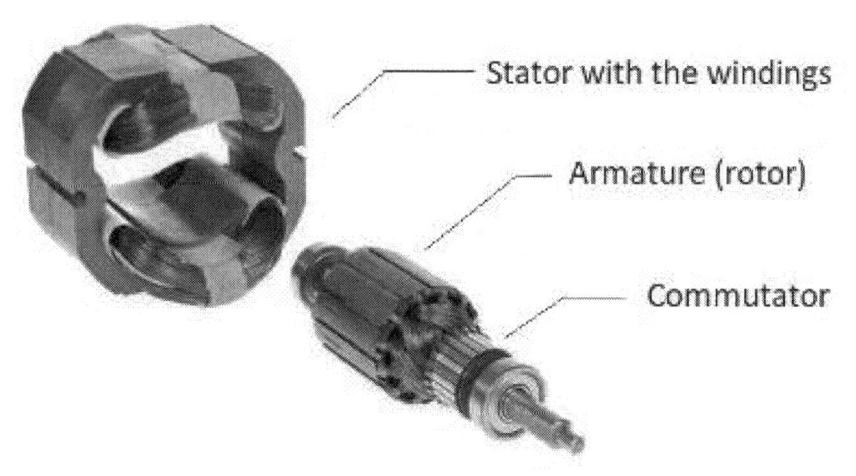

*Figure 6 How the parts fit together (P Xavier © 2019)*

Although these parts of the motor are essential, together they can be thought of as operating with just two parts. The magnet (or magnets) around the edge of the motor case that remains static, so it's called the **stator** of a motor. Inside the stator, there is the coil, mounted on an axle that spins around at high speed & this is called the **rotor**. The rotor also includes the commutator.

Increasing the turning power (torque) that is made by the motor can be achieved in a number of ways. The first is to use powerful permanent magnets, the second is to increase the electric current flowing through the windings & the third is to make the windings from many loops of very thin wire instead of one loop of thick wire.

## AC motors

All AC motors fall into two families, synchronous & asynchronous motors. The family tree for AC motors is shown in figure 7.

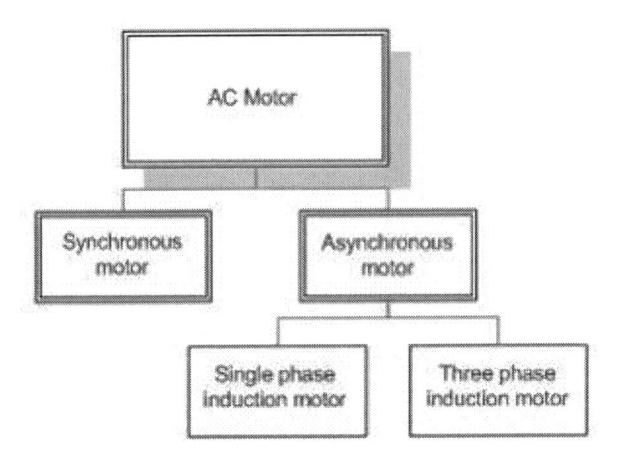

*Figure 7 The AC family tree (P Xavier © 2019)*

## The synchronous motor

These AC motors operate at a synchronous speed & convert AC electrical energy into mechanical power.

When the AC power is fed into the synchronous motor, a revolving field is set up. This revolving field will drag the rotor towards it but due to the inertia of the rotor, it can not. Therefore there is no starting torque. Because of this, the synchronous motor is not a self-starting motor. This AC motor has two electrical inputs. One is the stator winding which is supplied by a 3-phase supply & the other is to the rotor winding which is supplied by a DC supply. Thus, two magnetic fields are produced in a synchronous motor.

The 3 phase winding produces 3 phase magnetic flux & the rotor winding produces a constant flux. The 3 phase winding produces a magnetic field which rotates at a speed called a synchronous speed (hence the name of this motor).

When rotor & the stator start to rotate, at a certain point in time, both the rotor & the stator will have the same polarity which will cause a repulsive force on the rotor. Then, following this, they will have an attractive force. But rotor remains in standstill condition due to its high inertial moment. Therefore, the synchronous motor is not self-starting. This type of motor has the advantage of having a constant motor speed, irrespective of any applied load. Also, the electromagnetic power of this motor varies linearly with the voltage applied & when compared to an induction motor, it operates at much higher efficiencies at lower speeds.

However, it has some disadvantages. It is not a self-starting motor, therefore it does need an arrangement for starting & as the starting torque is zero, it cannot be started under a load. It is therefore used in applications such as conveyor belt systems.

## Asynchronous or induction motor

An induction motor is also called an asynchronous motor. This is because it runs at a speed lower than the synchronous speed. This motor can falls into two sub-categories. A single phase induction motor & a 3 phase induction motor.
With an asynchronous motor, the single armature winding will act as an armature winding & as a field winding.

The flux is produced within the air gap whenever the stator winding is supplied to the air gap. This flux will rotate at a fixed speed. Therefore, it will create a voltage in both the stator & the rotor winding. The current flow through the rotor winding reacts with the rotating flux & this is what produces the torque. When an AC electrical supply is fed to the stator winding within any induction motor, an alternating flux will be produced.
This flux rotates at an asynchronous speed & this flux is called the rotating magnetic field. Due to the relative speed between the stator rotating magnetic field & rotor conductor, an induced electro-magnetic field is developed within the rotor conductor.

A rotor current is then produced due to this induced electro magnetic field. The current lags behind the stator flux. The direction of this induced opposes the source of its production. The source of the production is the relative velocity between rotor stator flux & the rotor. The rotor will try to rotate in the same direction as a stator in order to reduce the relative velocity.

## Single phase induction motor

Any AC electrical motor that uses a single phase power supply is always called a single phase induction motor. It can be found in numerous domestic & industrial applications. It consists of a stator & a rotor. A single phase power supply is given to the stator winding. A squirrel cage rotor laminated with the iron core is connected to a mechanical load with the help of a shaft. When the single-phase supply is given to the stator winding an alternating flux will produce in the stator winding. Due to the rotating flux in the stator, an alternating electromagnetic field is induced within the rotor. However, the alternating flux does not provide the required rotation to the rotor. Therefore, single phase motors are not self-starting.

To make this motor self-starting, it needs to be temporarily converted into a two phase motor. This type of motor has the advantage of being lightweight & very efficient. The downsides are that it does not produce a uniform level of torque & the insulation costs are fairly high. These motors can typically be found in fridges, compressors & portable drills.

## Three phase induction motor

When a three phase electric supply is connected to a stator winding, the motor is called a three phase induction motor. As was seen in the single phase motor, the three phase motor has a stator & rotor winding.

Any stator wounded by a three phase winding, which is supplied by a three phase electrical current will produce an alternating flux which rotates at a synchronous speed. The rotating magnetic field creates an electro-magnetic field in the rotor which creates an induced current which flows in a direction which is opposite to the rotating magnetic field. This produces the torque in the rotor, but the speed of the rotor will not be equal to the stator.

If the speed matches the stator, no torque will be produced. These motors are simple & rugged, require minimal maintenance & offer both a high power factors & high efficiency. They are also self-starting. However, any increase in load will reduce the speed output & controlling the speed is somewhat difficult. They also have a poor starting torque.

These motors can typically be found in lathes. As was stated previously, AC motors are now becoming increasingly more popular & their use in EV's are now clearly outpacing the use of DC motors which were the standard in forklift trucks, electric milk floats & very early EV's. Of these AC motors, there are two main types that are currently favoured by car manufacturers.

## The AC induction motor & the permanent magnet motor

Tesla had traditionally used the AC induction motor as they are cheap to manufacture, cheap to maintain but suffer from low efficiency & low power density compared to a permanent magnet motor which provides a higher power density & very high efficiency. The downside is that the permanent magnet motors are more expensive, but Tesla has now moved to the AC permanent magnet motor for use with their model 3. This is because AC induction motors have to use electricity to generate magnetic currents inside the motor (this is what enables the rotor to spin), whereas a permanent magnet motor does not require any additional current as its magnets are always on.

This all means that the Model 3's motor is much more efficient & therefore better for smaller & lighter cars, but not ideal for high-performance cars, since an AC induction motor can produce greater power.

AC induction motors are therefore more suited to the higher end of the car market, whilst an AC permanent magnet motor lends itself to the smaller car market. This may not always be the case, as there is currently much research being undertaken in the field of electric motors & it is perfectly possible that another variant of the AC motor family may become better suited for use in the EV market. It may even be possible that an enhanced DC motor may once again become the 'go to motor' for EV manufacturers.

Permanent magnet motors, as their name suggest use permanent magnets rather than windings in the stator. The magnetic field is therefore permanent & consequently the entire design is more efficient than one that relies on windings.

Permanent magnets are made from hard ferromagnetic materials such as alnico & ferrite that are subjected to special processing within a very strong magnetic field during manufacture. This process aligns the internal microcrystalline structure of the metal which then makes it very hard to demagnetise afterwards.
The AC induction motor does not use permanent magnets; instead they have windings that are wrapped around a laminated iron magnetic core that form magnetic poles when they are energised with an electric current.
Now it is time to examine the DC motor.

## DC motors

All members of the DC motor family are shown in the following diagram.

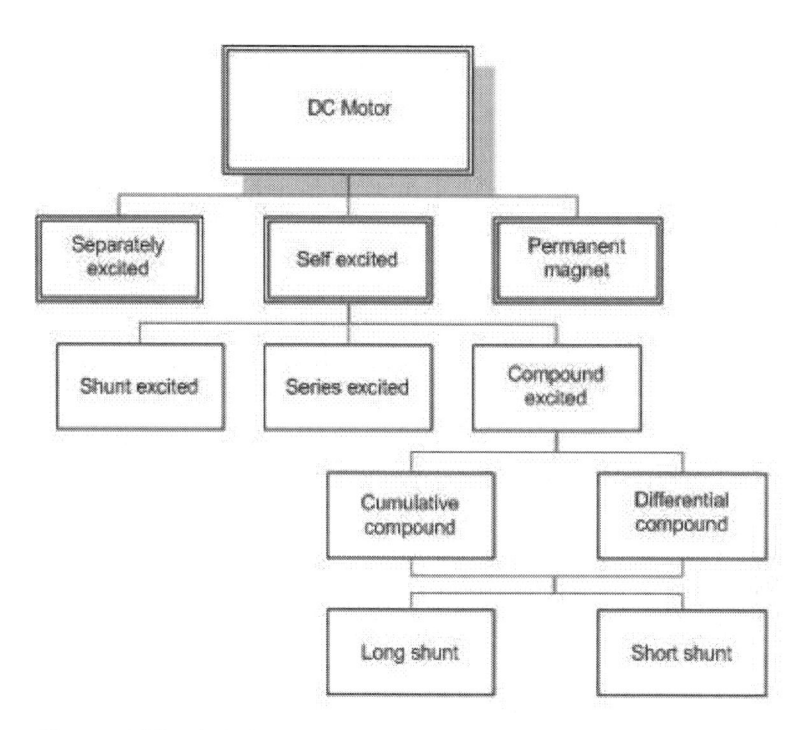

*Figure 8 The DC family tree (P Xavier © 2019)*

Every DC motor has the same six parts. The axle, the rotor, the commutator, magnets & brushes. The basic component of any DC motor is the current carrying armature which is connected to the electrical supply through the commutator & brushes. The armature is placed between two permanent magnets which produce a magnetic field.

The applied DC converts the electrical energy into the mechanical energy because of two magnetic fields which interact. One field is produced by the permanent magnet whilst the other is produced by the electric current flowing through the winding. These two interacting magnetic fields cause the rotor to turn. In a nutshell, that is how the DC motor works.

## Separately Excited DC Motors (SEDC)

In all DC motors, there is a stator which is the static part. This is made up of winding. Inside this is the rotor which is the moving & is made from the armature winding. In a separately excited DC motor, separate power is given to both the field & the armature windings.

These field windings are energised by a separate DC source as the armature current does not flow through the field windings. Therefore, these coils are separately isolated from each other & this is what differentiates this motor from the others.

There are three different methods to control the speed of this motor. Field control, field rheostat or by an armature control. This motor can easily ran in reverse by switching the polarity of the field & the speed can be controlled by using a variable DC electric supply.

## Permanent Magnet DC Motors (PMDC)

With a permanent magnet DC motors, the magnetic field is created by the permanent magnet. It consists of an armature winding & a stator, but does not contain the field winding. In this kind of DC motor, the field flux is produced by a radially magnetised permanent magnet which is placed on the inner edge of the stator core.
The magnets are arranged so that the North Pole & the South Pole are arranged alternately & facing towards the armature. They are simple & efficient motors that are used for small kW applications such as wheel chairs, windscreen motors & ICE car starter motors.

## Shunt Wound DC Motor (SWDM)

In these DC motors, the field winding is connected in parallel to the armature winding. Therefore a full voltage is applied across the field winding. It is made up of a large number of windings & they have a high resistance. Because of this, a small current is needed during operation & also needed to start the motor. These motors are not suitable for variable speed drives & they require brushes. They are typically found in lathes & centrifugal pumps.

## Series Wound DC Motor (SWDM)

In this DC motor, the field winding is connected internally in a series to the armature winding. The motor consists of a stator housing the field winding & a rotor carrying the armature conductor. The field winding has fewer turns & thicker dimensions which provide the minimum resistance to the full armature current. This has the advantage of allowing this motor to be used in high torque applications & allows a very low starting current, but as the speed decreases, so does the torque. They can typically be found in lifts & conveyors.

## Compound Wound DC Motor (CWDM)

Compound wound DC motors all fall within the family of self excited DC motors. In this motor, there are two sets of field windings. One set is connected in series with the armature winding & the second is connected in parallel to the armature winding. It is basically a combination of the SWDM & SWDC, but they have the advantage of providing enhanced properties of both those motors.

This type of motor can be further subdivided into long shunt & short shunt motors. In the long shunt variant, the field winding is connected in parallel across the armature & series field coil, whilst in the short shunt, the field winding is only connected the armature winding.

These motors are ideally suited to heavy loads as they have a high level of torque & speed, but have the drawback of needing high maintenance. They are typically found in lifts & conveyors.

## Series or parallel again

If you watch F1, you may be familiar with the term 'drivetrain'. If you are not familiar with the term, it can be defined as the collection of individual components that deliver power (from an ICE, electric motor or both) to the vehicle's wheels.

In hybrid electric vehicles, the design of the drivetrain determines exactly how the electric motor works in conjunction with the ICE. The drivetrain will affect the mechanical efficiency, the fuel consumption & also the ultimate purchase price of the vehicle.

Hybrid vehicles that use a series drivetrain will only receive their mechanical power from the electric motor, where it can be powered either by the battery, or the ICE. In hybrids that use a parallel drivetrain, the electric motor & the ICE can both provide mechanical power simultaneously. Vehicles with a series/parallel drivetrain allow both the ICE & electric motor to provide power either independently or in conjunction with the other.

Both conventional hybrids & plug-in hybrids have various models that have series, parallel & also series/parallel drivetrains.

## Series drivetrains

A series drivetrain is the simplest configuration for a hybrid vehicle. In a series hybrid vehicle the electric motor is the only means of providing power to the wheels. The electric motor can receive its electrical power from either the battery pack or from the ICE. A computer will determine exactly how much of the power comes from the battery or from the ICE. Both the ICE & regenerative braking will & can charge the battery.

A hybrid with a series drivetrain will offer its best performance in stop & go traffic as during this operation the ICE is very inefficient, therefore the on board computer will opt to power the electric motor solely from the battery, therefore saving the ICE for conditions where it is more efficient.

The ICE is usually smaller in vehicles that utilise a series drivetrain as it only has to meet certain power demands; therefore the battery is generally more powerful to make up for the undersized ICE.

## Parallel drivetrains

In all parallel hybrid vehicle drivetrains, the ICE & the electric motor work together in tandem to generate the electrical energy that drives the wheels, the battery is usually smaller than those in series drivetrains so they rely on regenerative braking to help keep the batteries charged. In addition to this, when the vehicle's power demand is low, they will also use the ICE to charge the battery. Exactly like an alternator in ICE vehicles.

As the electric motor has a direct connection to the wheels in parallel drivetrains, the inefficiency of converting mechanical power to electricity & back is greatly reduced, which will increase the overall efficiency of these hybrids.

## Series/Parallel drivetrains

The concept of the series/parallel drivetrain marries the pros & cons of both the parallel & series drivetrains. But, by combining the two concepts, the ICE can drive the wheels directly (as was seen in the parallel drivetrain) but also it can be completely disconnected, allowing the electric motor to provide the energy (as was seen in the series drivetrain). The Toyota Prius paved the way in making the series/parallel drivetrain a viable design. The series/parallel drivetrain will allow petrol only & electric only periods, allowing the ICE to operate at optimum efficiency during certain periods. At low speeds it will operate more like as a series drivetrain vehicle, but at high speeds, when the series drivetrain is less efficient, the ICE takes over & the energy loss is minimised.

This combined system does cost more than a parallel hybrid as it requires a generator, a much larger battery along with a more powerful computer to control this combined system. This can be offset as the greater efficiency will offset the higher purchase cost as it will use much less fuel than the series or parallel system vehicles would require.

## Drivetrain inertia

Firstly, it was previously stated that the most efficient & therefore ideal use of an electric motor would be to have one powering each wheel. The reason for this is due to what is known as drivetrain inertia.

To explain what this is, imagine a traditional ICE powered vehicle, where the power from the engine is transferred through the clutch & the gear box through to the rear axle via a crank shaft. Each of these elements spin due to the power from the engine that is translated into torque. However, as each of these components turn, energy is wasted.

Therefore, the longer the chain of components between the power source & the wheels, the greater the degree of inertia that will be experienced which means the greater the loss of power. A percentage of the power will therefore always be lost between the engine & the wheels. If the inertia causes a 10% loss, then 10% more fuel will be needed to compensate for that loss.

To overcome this, an electric motor can be placed at each wheel. This therefore means there is no drivetrain inertia as the motors drive the wheels directly & as there are no components in between, there is no loss in energy.

However, currently BEV's use two designs. Those which utilise a single electric motor design & those that have a two motor configuration (one on each axle). The single electric motor will therefore suffer from a greater loss of power than the EV's that use two motors, purely because there are more components between the motor & the wheel that resist the power. But the optimal design would be to have a motor at each wheel because there are no mechanical connections between the motor & the wheel which will create inertia. Therefore, when the cost of electric motors reduces over time, it will become commonplace for EV's to utilise a four electric motor design, one electric motor placed at each wheel.

# Chapter 5 – **AC, DC & electronics**

So far in this book, there has been much talk about **Direct Current** (DC) & **Alternating Current** (AC) with regard to electricity & the components in an EV. To understand why this is important, it is worth looking at what AC & DC is.

You already know that all EV's have a battery. In fact every battery ever made gives up its power as DC electricity, which is fine if the motor you are using in your EV is a DC motor as it will require DC electricity to operate, but as we have seen, the majority of electric motors used in EV's are now AC motors. These do not work with DC electricity, they require AC electricity. Therefore there is a slight problem that will need to be overcome before AC motors can be used in an EV.

Also, if you are reading this in North America, the electricity supply in your home is DC, so charging the battery in an EV at home may not be a big problem, but in the majority of the electrified world, domestic electricity is AC, so it is worth knowing what the difference between AC & DC electricity is & what to do when you need one, not the other.

## AC/DC

As has been previously stated, electricity is just the flow of electrons from one place to another. For instance, from a battery to a motor. These electrons travel from the negative pole (-) towards the positive pole (+). This is the current. This can be demonstrated in figure 9, where it can be seen that the DC flow is moving directly & in one direction (if viewed on an oscilloscope).

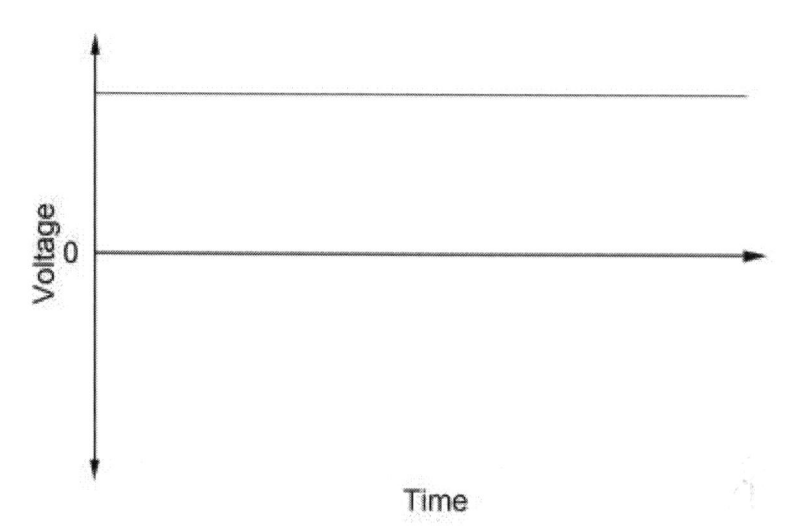

*Figure 9 DC electricity viewed in an oscilloscope (P Xavier © 2017)*

The grey line can be seen travelling in a direct line from left to right over time. If this is compared to an AC current, the difference is plainly evident.

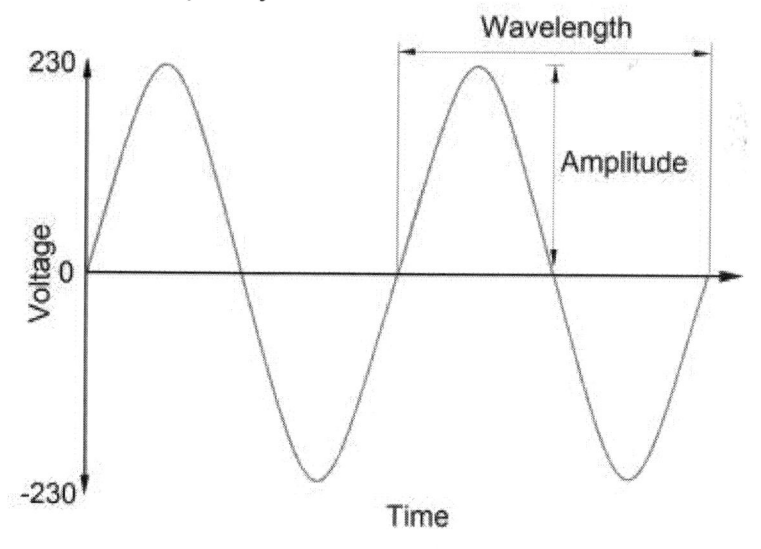

*Figure 10 AC electricity viewed in an oscilloscope (P Xavier © 2017)*

Now, an AC current can be observed to be travelling from left to right (as before), but now it is constantly changing direction as it follows the pattern of a sine wave (when viewed through an oscilloscope). The wavelength is the time it takes for the current to complete 1 cycle. That is moving from 0 to +230v, back through 0 towards -230v & back again to 0. The standard for electrical appliances in the UK & Europe is generally 50 or 60Hz (Hertz), therefore the current cycles 50 or 60 times every second.

The characteristics of DC electricity is that it cannot travel very far before it begins to lose energy; the flow causes steady magnetism along the electrical wiring; the frequency of DC is always zero; DC flows in only one direction within a circuit; the current is always of a constant magnitude; the flow of electrons are always moving in one direction; a DC current is obtained from batteries as these provide DC electricity; the passive parameter is resistance; the power factor is always 1 & DC electricity can be pure or pulsating.

The comparable characteristics of AC is that an AC voltage can travel over a greater distance without any significant loss of energy; the flow causes a rotating magnet along a wire; the frequency of AC is 50Hz or 60Hz depending upon the country; the AC voltage reverses direction whilst flowing in a circuit, the current of magnitude will vary over time; the flow of electrons switch over time – backwards & forwards; an AC current is obtainable from the majority of the worlds mains electricity; the passive parameter is impedance; the power factor lies between 0 & 1; AC electricity can be sinusoidal (as in figure 10), trapezoidal, triangular or even square.

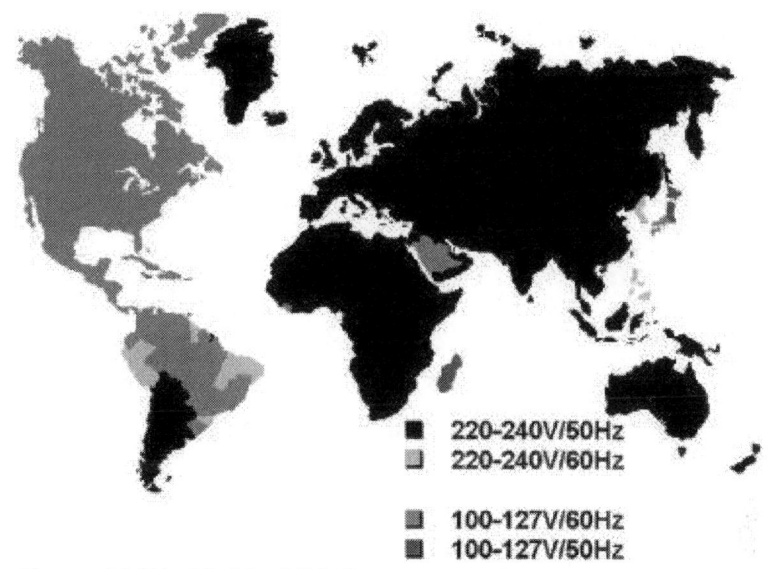

*Figure 11 Worldwide AC/DC standards (Public Domain Image © 2006)*

Therefore the characterisation for both DC & AC are very different. The electrical current from an EV's batteries will always be DC. Therefore to charge the batteries in the majority of the electrified world in a domestic situation, an AC current, at 230v & cycling at 50Hz will need to be converted to a DC current. The AC/DC 'standard' differs across various countries. The map shown here in figure 11 shows which geographical areas use which voltage/Hz.

Therefore it can be seen that the majority of the world's electricity network is based on 220 – 240v at either 50Hz or 60Hz. Although the voltage being supplied by the National Grid in the UK averages at 242v, therefore most domestic appliances are running at a voltage higher than needed.

The voltage in the UK is also provided as three phase. That is three phases of electricity all using the electrical cabling at the same time, therefore it can & is split into three separate feeds before it arrives at a property. It is typical that several houses are fed by one phase, whilst the neighbouring houses to one side use another phase, & those on the other side use the third phase. A three phase AC supply looks like this.

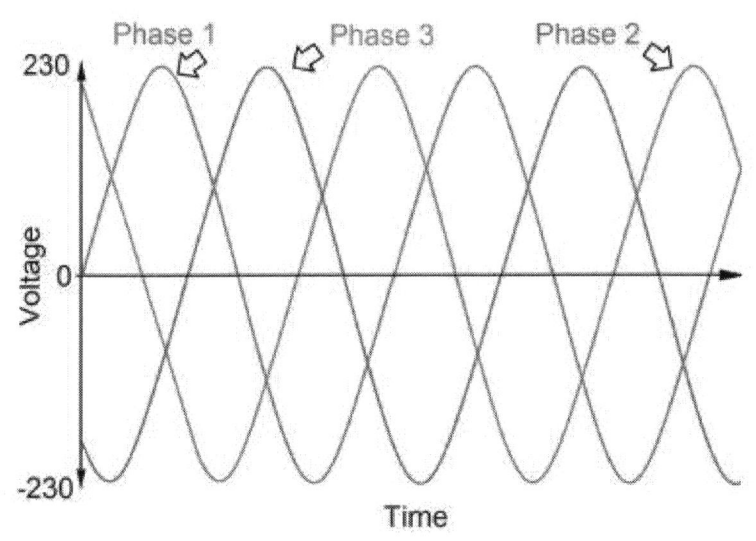

*Figure 12 Three phase AC current (P Xavier © 2017)*

Here a three phase AC current can be observed to be travelling from left to right (as before), but now three distinct phases are sharing the same cable, but all three are slightly out of sync allowing them to share the same space.

# Electronics

Regardless whether you have access to AC or DC electricity, there is electronics built into the EV or hybrid that will convert the electrical supply to the type that is needed by the vehicle. Each of these functions will now be looked at in turn.

### Rectifier

A rectifier converts AC electrical power to DC electrical power & this is embedded inside all EV's & hybrids. This is used to convert an AC domestic supply of electricity into DC electricity, which enables the batteries to be charged during the 'plugged in' charging period.

## Inverter

EV's & hybrids also have an inverter. The inverter changes DC electrical energy to AC electrical energy & is used to convert the DC supply from the batteries to feed the AC motors. This is also embedded inside all EV's & hybrids. The inverter is also used during regenerative braking, when it feeds electrical energy back to the battery. As previously stated, the kinetic energy of the decelerating vehicle is converted into electricity in the motor, & then sent back to the battery pack for later use via the inverter. Each motor will therefore need a dedicated inverter. Therefore if the vehicle has two motors (one at each axle), then there will need to be two inverters, or one, where all the electricity cables are routed through.

## Converter

A converter is also needed. A 'step up converter' increases the voltage to the level required & a 'step down converter' decreases the voltage to the required level.

## Tandem unit

An EV typically has the inverter & converter housed in a single unit & this is called a tandem unit. These units therefore handle the electrical throughput in the EV or hybrid. The inverter/converter supplies the electrical current to the battery pack for recharging during regenerative braking & it also provides electricity to the motor for the vehicle propulsion. EV's & hybrids tend to use relatively low voltage DC batteries (approximately 210 volts to keep the physical size of the batteries to a minimum), but conversely, they tend to use high voltage AC motors (approximately 650 volts). Therefore the inverter/converter unit converts the different voltages when needed allowing the voltage discrepancy to operate together seamlessly.

## Battery Management System (BMS)

As has been seen earlier, the preferred battery chemistry for EV's is lithium ion, however, as the internal chemistry is reactive to the elements & sensitive to heat, each of the cells need to be monitored. This is achieved with a 'battery management system' (BMS). During the charging period, the BMS ensures that each of the cells have the same voltage level (typically +/- 0.01 volts). Without a BMS, it would be possible for one individual cell to overcharge & this could cause an explosion or fire. During the discharge period, without a BMS controlling the battery, it is possible for one individual cell to underperform. This would have the result of the other cells in a module to be drained too quickly or at too high a rate, which would again cause an explosion or fire, or at best damage the affected cells. Therefore, the BMS has to keep track of hundreds or even thousands of individual battery cells to ensure that they give & receive a safe & controlled amount of electricity.

All Li-Ion batteries are fitted with their own inbuilt battery management system (BMS). This will need to communicate effectively with any other onboard charge controller to enable reconnections if any disconnections occur. This can happen when the batteries state of charge (SOC) drops below a certain threshold, the BMS will disconnect the battery to avoid damage occurring to it. This is called low voltage disconnect (LVD). They will also disconnect to avoid over-charging. If reconnection did not occur at a later point in time, that battery will fail to be recharged. It is therefore imperative that any charge controller used onboard is designed to liaise with the Li-Ion BMS if Li-Ion batteries are used to power the vehicle.

## Controller

The controller is the part of the electronic system that acts as a brain, a bridge or a gate between each of the components. For instance, in an ICE vehicle, the accelerator pedal is mechanical & opens a flap in the engine to allow more air into the combustion chamber. This is not the case with an EV.

Instead, the pressure on the accelerator pedal is monitored by the controller, the harder it is pressed, the more electricity is given to the electric motor/s, which therefore results in greater speed. Therefore it acts as an interface between the driver & the machine, interpreting the controls & then directing the vehicles components.

It will oversee all the other electronic components, such as instructing the inverter on just how it is to perform. Much work is spent fine tuning the control unit to achieve the best simulation of an ICE that is possible for the driver.
The controller can therefore be thought of as the brain for the whole vehicle. The other electronics can & do work independently, but are all under the direct control of the controller.

All these electronic components work hard & therefore tend to generate a lot of heat. To counter this, the electronic components are also fitted with their own independent cooling system, complete with pumps & radiators, which are all completely independent to the vehicles own cooling system. Many vehicles also incorporate this cooling system into the batteries so that the electronics will heat the batteries when the ambient temperature is low.

# Chapter 6 – **Cables, connections & power**

As was previously stated, when it comes to charging an EV, there are numerous charging modes & types of power sources as well as numerous connection plugs on the cables. It is therefore important that these are fully understood or any owner of an EV may find themselves unable to drive because their vehicle has not had a sufficient charge or unable to drive as the battery has been cooked & therefore find themselves looking at a hefty garage bill to replace the batteries.

It is not as simple as plugging the car into the nearest outlet as there are numerous factors to consider. Do you have the correct plug, is it the correct type of outlet. Do you have enough time to achieve the level of charge that you require? Tesla uses its own proprietary charging standard that is not compatible with the majority of the charging network, therefore are there Tesla chargers on your route if you require them? It is clearly not as simple as the EV manufacturers will lead you to believe. For instance, if you are charging the vehicle at home (80% of EV charging happens at home), then the standard electrical output found in your home will not provide the vehicle with a full charge, even after an overnight 8 hour of charge. A dedicated power supply will therefore need to be fitted to allow you to achieve a full charge overnight. In addition, a suitable place will need to be found to do this, such as a garage or car port.

Therefore, it will be advantageous to look at the numerous options that are available when charging your EV.

## Charge modes

There are currently four methods available, although sometimes mode 1 is ignored & mode 2 through to 4 are numbered 1 to 3. This is all due to the lack of a definitive standard.

### Mode 1

Mode 1 is not an officially recognised. This is because it is not a safe method of charging an EV as it does not use any standard charging units or leads supplied by EV or charge point manufacturers.

Mode 1 is when someone charges an EVB using their own charging leads that are connected to their home power supply. This practice is not recommended in the UK or EEC as it has the potential for not being safe & could also invalidate the warranty on an EV.

### Mode 2

Mode 2 uses a 13 amp charging lead that can deliver only the slowest speed of charge. It is when you plug into a standard household 13 amp socket (for instance the ones found in your home in the UK or EEC). The vehicle plug on the end of the lead must have the correct type of connector that fits your chosen EV. A Mode 2 charging lead will typically be provided with your vehicle.

In UK & EEC this is 230VAC 6A, whilst in North America the DC output can be converted to 115VAC 15A. This singe phase supply will produce approximately 1.5kW & the charge time will be in the region of 7 to 30 hours depending on the battery size on the EV. Level 1 will only meet the overnight charging requirement for e-bikes, e-scooters, electric wheelchairs & PHEV's that do not exceed 12kWh.

## Mode 3

This is the most common method for charging EV's. This method uses a dedicated charge point that is either installed at home, at work place or in a public space such as a car park. EV manufacturers recommend this as their preferred solution for charging EV's. In a domestic installation these can be installed with a fixed lead or a (standard) 7 pin electric vehicle charging socket which can be used by EV's. Therefore the point can be used by any visiting friends or family who also own an EV.

Alternatively, if a fixed cable is not fitted, then it is important that you obtain one, but it would need to be the same lead that you can plug into your EV. This will also double up as the one used when you charge in at work or in public, but it is not uncommon for these points to have a fixed lead.

Domestic installations that use Mode 3 chargers are typically wall mounted 230VAC 30A, two pole chargers. These can charge a medium sized EV in 4 to 5 hours. These will produce approximately 7kW. Domestic properties that use a mode 3 charger should charge their EV only following periods of heavy use, such as cooking, clothes washing, clothes drying to prevent the chance of overloading the power supply.

## Mode 4

This is currently the most powerful charging mode available at a charge point. It is powered by a DC current, which will charge at the fastest rapid speed of charge possible using a tethered lead. Only vehicles with a Mode 4 vehicle inlet connector type can use this type of charge point.

Mode 4 DC Rapid chargers were traditionally 50kW, however there are DC Rapid chargers available that will provide power from 22kW up to 400kW. Some are being developed to provide 600kW & able to provide a short high powered boost using flash charging for 15-20 seconds.

This is all possible as they bypass the on board battery charger & feed the power directly to the battery. The battery charger is therefore provided within the charging point. They can charge a Li-Ion battery to 80 percent within approximately 30 minutes, but this level of power demand is equal to five average UK households.

## Charging cables & their plugs

The vehicle power inlets will vary from manufacturer to manufacturer with EV's & hybrids. Currently EV's will come with either a Type 1 or a Type 2 inlet, but some manufacturers also offer the option to add an additional second inlet (called a CHAdeMO) to allow that vehicle to be charged from a more powerful rapid speed charge point & therefore charged at a faster speed.

In addition, EV's are now coming onto the market fitted with another type of combined socket which is called a CCS Combo. This has the benefit of allowing the EV to be charged via a slow point, a fast point & even some more powerful rapid charge points.

## Type 1 - J1772 (Yazaki connector)

This is 5 pin AC connector that is generally found on American & Asian vehicles. It carries a maximum 230V AC 32 amp single phase (7.4kW) electrical supply.

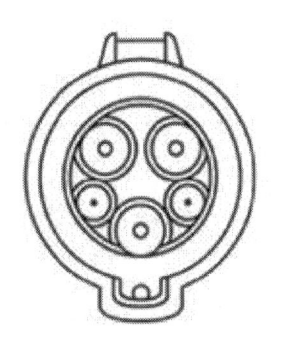

The Society of Automotive Engineers (SAE) have issued document *J1772 – Recommended Practice for Electric Vehicle and Hybrid Electric Vehicle Conductive Charge* which sets standards for the charging cable, connector & vehicle socket for plug-in EV's. Currently all EVs sold in both the United States & Canada comply with J1772 standards for both AC Level 1 & AC Level 2 charging.

The type 1 connector is currently found in the Mitsubishi Outlander PHEV, Nissan LEAF & Vauxhall Ampera.

## Rapid charging CHAdeMO

CHAdeMO is the trade name of a quick charging method for EV's, delivering up to 62.5 kW of high-voltage DC via a special electrical connector. CHAdeMO was the first DC rapid charging connector & is typically found on vehicles originating in Asia, especially Japan. It is constructed with a 2 pin DC connector which can carry a maximum 230V DC, 63 amp three phase (62.5 kW) electrical supply. The DC fast charging of these cars is performed using a special connector that was jointly developed by the Tokyo Electric Power Company & Mitsubishi.

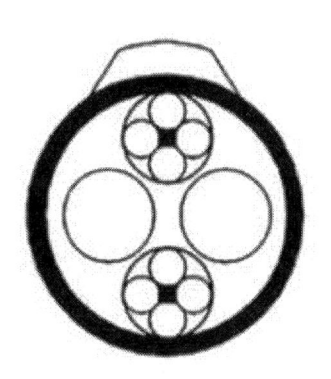

DC Level 3 fast charging is a relatively recent development & it is currently found in the United States & Canada only on the Nissan LEAF & the Mitsubishi iMiEV. CHAdeMO is a name created by combining letters from the Japanese words that mean "charge for moving". The CHAdeMO standard has now been implemented by several Japanese manufacturers.

## Type 2 – IEC62196 (Mennekes connector)

This uses a 7 pin AC connector & it is found on European vehicles. It carries a maximum 400V AC 63 amp, 3 phase (43kW) electric supply. In January 2013, the IEC 62196 Type 2 connector was selected by the European Commission as the official charging plug to use within the EEC. Since then it has been adopted as the recommended connector in several other countries outside the EEC, including New Zealand.

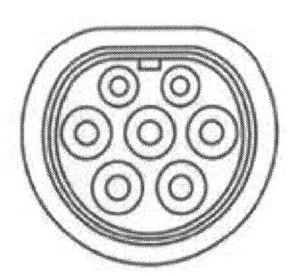

It is used in EV's such as the Audi A3 e-tron, the BMW i3 & the Volvo V60 PHEV. Some manufacturers now offer an option to add an additional second inlet which will allow the Type 2 socket to also accept a rapid speed charge. This is called a CCS Combo.

## CCS Combo

This is an extension of the type 2 connector & is called the 'combined charging system' (CCS). The CCS allows mode 3 charging by connecting just to the upper circular receptacle. Mode 4 charging can be achieved with a plug that includes the top part & the two DC terminals (the bottom two pins).

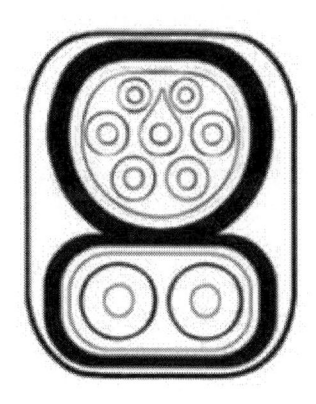

Currently the manufactures that support CCS include: BMW, Daimler, Fiat Chrysler, Ford, General Motors, Hyundai, Jaguar, Kia, Renault, Tesla & Volkswagen. In the United States, BMW & VW claim that the East Coast & West Coast corridors now have complete CCS networks installed. The CCS will provide the following levels of charge:

AC level 1: 120VAC 12–16A up to 1.92kW.
AC level 2: 240VAC 80A 19.2kW.
DC level 1: 200-500VDC up to 80A (40kW).
DC level 2: 200-500VDC up to 200A (100kW).

## The trouble with Tesla

Tesla Motors do not follow the standards that are currently available. They have therefore developed their own system. Their 'supercharger' can charge a depleted battery to 80% in 40 minutes to give a driving range of 270km (charging the last 20% from 80 - 100% will double the charge time).

Tesla are allegedly in discussions with Nissan & BMW, with the aim of offering their supercharger to these EV manufacturers. They are also working on an inter protocol charging adapter that can support the CHAdeMO & CCS systems.

Charging the Tesla S 85 with a Tesla supercharger starts with a voltage of approximately 375V at 240A, which consumes 90kW. As the battery starts to charge, the voltage rises to approximately 390VDC, whilst the current will drop to 120A.

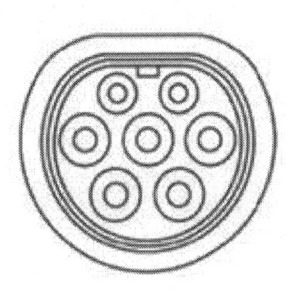

The Tesla S 85 uses a type 2 connector (on UK & EEC models), as does the Model X & Model 3. However, there is an adapter available that enables a Tesla 3 owner to use a CHAdeMO socket. The new Model Y has a type 2 connector along with CCS (in the UK & EEC).

## Simplified charging

With all these modes & types, it would be a little confusing for anyone; therefore it can be simplified slightly. Everything can be grouped into slow charging, fast charging & rapid charging.

### Slow charging (3kW)

Slow charging of an EV will be achieved using one of the following:

    3-pin 3kW AC
    Type 1 3kW AC
    Type 2 3kW AC
    Commando 3kW AC

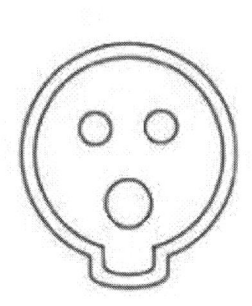

The commando is a cable type not previously listed. It can be thought of as a UK or EEC domestic cable & plug, but it has a slightly different plug to the standard UK plug. Anyone who works in industry or a building site may be familiar with this type of plug as it is often used for DC equipment such as 110v power tools.

Slow charging is the most common method of charging an EV. In most cases a standard single phase 13 Amp three-pin plug is used to draw up to 3kW of power. A full charge may typically take 6 to 8 hours. While the first wave of publicly accessible on-street charge points were of this type, these are now being replaced by fast & rapid units. Nearly all EV's can be slow charged. Each vehicle is supplied with a charging cable with the appropriate connectors & cable; typically a standard 3-pin plug for the charging point outlet & either a Type 1 or 7-pin Type 2 (Mennekes) connector for plugging into the vehicle side.

## Fast charging (7-22kW)

Fast charging of an EV will be achieved using one of the following:

> Type 2 7-22kW AC
> Type 1 7kW AC
> Commando 7-22kW AC

Fast charging reduces the EV charge time by half when compared to the slow charge. It achieves this by doubling the available current to 32 amps (7kW), which means that a full charge may take 3 or 4 hours. A large number of commercial & many public on-street chargers use this technology; therefore it is likely that this charge rate will become more common & used to replace the network of public slow charging points across the UK & in the EEC.

Being less common, achieving fast three phase charging is also technically possible, with each phase delivering approximately 7kW to deliver a total of 22kW. While not all EV's are able to accept a 1-phase fast charge at 32 amps (7kW), most can be connected to them (with the right connector) & will draw either 13 or 32 amps depending on their capability. Type 1 connectors were initially the most common type used at the charger end; these are now being replaced by the more versatile Type 2 (Mennekes) connector.

## Rapid AC charging (up to 43kW)

Rapid AC chargers provide a high power AC power supply with power ratings up to 43kW. At this level of power, an EV can typically be charged to 80% in less than half an hour. The Rapid AC option is a new development & only available on one or two EV models in the UK. The more common rapid charging station is rapid DC unit. Due to their high power, rapid AC units are equipped with a tethered cable which is equipped with a non removable Type 2 (Mennekes) connector.

## Rapid DC charging (up to 50kW)

Rapid DC chargers provide a high power DC power supply with power ratings up to 50kW. At this level of power, an EV can typically be charged to 80% in less than half an hour. This is the most common type of rapid charging unit. Rapid DC chargers are equipped with a tethered cable with a non-removable connector which is coupled with an appropriate inlet socket which is fitted to some compatible EV models. Rapid DC chargers are fitted with either a CHAdeMO or 9-pin CCS connector plug at the vehicle end. Tesla superchargers are also rapid DC chargers & will charge at around 120 kW.

However, no matter which charging method is adopted, it is likely that the promised level of charge may not be attainable, just as some Nissan LEAF owners found out.

## A note on the LEAF

The media have reported that there have been many Nissan LEAF owners complaining that the range they were promised to achieve with their LEAF has not been achievable. So many people have complained in the UK that, the Advertising Standards Authority (ASA) is now considering whether to launch a formal investigation into the issue.

The whole problem has arisen because Nissan told their LEAF buyers that using rapid chargers would only take 40 minutes 'in moderate driving conditions' to achieve an 80% charge. They have now changed that claim to between 40 - 60 minutes.

There appears to be no issues with the first two charges on any given day. The first at home, then the first rapid charge en-route. But when drivers charge for the third time (or the second rapid charge), they face an excessively long wait. Therefore, this will affect any journey in a LEAF of more than 250 miles.

This unexpected extra time spent charging the LEAF could cost the motorist not only many wasted hours at a service station, but also many pounds in unforeseen parking fees & charging fees at a public charger.

Originally Nissan quoted a range of 235 miles for the LEAF, which they claim was derived by the measurement outlined in the New European Driving Cycle (NEDC), however, due to all the negative publicity regarding this range/charging issue, they have modified the range & now claim the LEAF has a range of 168 miles which they have now derived from the Worldwide Harmonised Light vehicle Test Procedure (WLTP). That is a drop of 67 miles.

This change in marketing may still be an issue for drivers who bought the LEAF under false pretences, & as this charging 'issue' has still not been resolved, it will also now be a potential problem for anyone who wishes to sell or purchase a LEAF.

## Current developments in battery technologies

The major problem currently cited with EV's is always the range of the vehicle. This problem can therefore be split into two issues, which are interrelated. Solving these two issues will automatically solve the range issue.

The first issue is the battery technology; the second is charging technologies. If the battery could hold ten times as much charge & be charged in minutes, not hours, then the range problem would be solved. Therefore there are boffins all over the world that are working on improving the batteries & also improving the charge times.

As there is so much research being undertaken in the field of batteries, it is impossible to mention every area, therefore only a small number will be mentioned here. Also, it is also impossible to predict the future; therefore the following areas may never become the battery technology that will transform the range of EV's from 200 kilometres to 2,000 kilometres on a single charge.

## Magnesium batteries

These batteries with an Mg chemistry could theoretically compete with Li-Ion's if they were rechargeable. Work is therefore being undertaken to make these batteries chargeable.

## Paper-polymer batteries

Another area that is generating much excitement is microbial bio-batteries as they are cheap, environmentally friendly & self-sustainable. Currently they suffer from low performance, so this is a hurdle that will need to be overcome before these batteries become common place.

## Silicon-based batteries

Li-Ion batteries use graphite anodes, but research is being undertaken on silicon anodes. Silicon anodes bind 25 times better than graphite anodes so a battery can hold 25 times more energy, but they suffer from low electrical conductivity, therefore this will need to be overcome before silicon batteries can become commercially available & commercially viable.

## Room-temperature sodium sulfur (RT-NaS) batteries

Sodium sulphur batteries have similar physical & chemical properties to Na & Li-Ion batteries. But need a high temperature (>300°C) to operate. Therefore there is research being undertaken to achieve a battery that works at room temperature.

## Nickel-zinc batteries

This battery chemistry is cheap, safe, nontoxic & environmentally friendly batteries that could compete with Li-Ion batteries for energy storage. However, they suffer from low life cycles. Their useable life will therefore need to be greatly increased before they become suitable for use.

## Potassium-ion batteries

Recently there has been a lot of work on improving the electrochemical performance of potassium-ion batteries, but there has not (so far) been a break through that will make a battery based on this chemistry viable.

## Salt-water batteries

Water will conduct ions & can therefore be used to form rechargeable batteries. However, the chemical stability of water lasts up to 2.3 V, which is three times less than Li-Ion batteries. Therefore this will need to be increased before they become suitable for use.

## Proton batteries

There is currently much research being undertaken in the field of high-performance proton exchange membrane (PEM) fuel cells. However their viability has been a challenge due to their high cost & problems encountered with the storage of hydrogen gas.

## Aluminium-ion batteries

The internal chemistry if this battery is cheap & readily available, but the batteries are not commercially viable at the moment.

There is much talk & hype regarding solid state batteries. All current batteries use liquid or a gel electrolyte. A solid state battery replaces the wet components with a solid that can operate in the same way as the wet chemistry. The chances are that these solid state batteries may become the next step in the evolution of batteries.

# Current developments in battery charging technologies

An evolution in charging is also needed to increase the usefulness of BEV's. Currently, all EV's need charging before they can be driven & may need to be recharged during a journey if the journey is longer than the range of the vehicle.

Therefore there is also a race to develop a more convenient method of doing this. Given the fact that 80% of EV charging happens at home, any development in charging will ultimately be installed in people's homes first. A likely candidate would be a high powered charging station that would be capable of delivering a minimum of 450kW.

## Ultra fast charging

Despite Tesla pushing their supercharger which operates at 150 kW, which can charge some cars in about an hour. Their supercharger, which operates up to 120 kW, can charge a Tesla to about 80% in about 30 minutes. Rival EV manufacturers are working on their own so there are currently developments in the pipeline regarding ultra fast charging of EV's. One developed by BMW & Porsche is said to allow up to 62 miles (100km) of charge in just three minutes, & 15 minutes for a full charge (10-80 % State of Charge (SOC)), which is twice as fast as Tesla's supercharger, but there are no EV's that are currently available that can utilise this charger to achieve these impressive charge rates.

Currently, the Audi e-tron is able to charge from 0 to 80% SOC in around 30 minutes using 150kW. Their next step which they propose to introduce with the Audi e-tron GT is expected to be charged to 80% SOC in 12 minutes with a charge of 350kW.

Currently, as there is no accepted global standard, every manufacturer, electrical company & many universities are individually developing systems. As such, there is currently a charging war in progress & it is anyone's guess as to what & who will win. Until there is an overall winner, alternative systems will come & go, which means that an expensive EV purchase may wasted if it houses a recharging system that becomes obsolete.

## Inductive charging

This would do away with the cables & the various connections. It works exactly the same way as some mobile phones. That is wireless charging that uses an electromagnetic field to transfer energy between two objects through electromagnetic induction.

Newer mobile phones can now be charged on a dedicated charge stand rather than being physically plugged into the phone charger. With regard to EV's, the charger is imbedded into the ground typically in a parking bay. When an EV fitted with induction charging pads on the underside is parked in the bay, it receives a charge that charges the battery.

This method has the benefit of not needing a physical connection to the vehicle, but the vehicle needs to be placed accurately in the bay & the technology is fairly expensive. Currently there is not an established standard for this wireless charging technology, so again an expensive EV purchase may be wasted if it houses a recharging system that becomes obsolete. It is rumoured that both BMW & Mercedes are set to include this technology to some of their upcoming car fleet. An offshoot of this inductive charging technology is being looked at where these hidden chargers are embedded within the road network, which would allow an EV to charge whilst it is being driven. This would reduce the charging time as the vehicle would charge on the go & therefore keep topping up the battery. Qualcomm have developed such a system called 'dynamic wireless charging' which they claim can charge a vehicle when it is travelling up to 70mph. However, so far, the system is only fitted to a 100 metre test road in France, where an electrically live coil is buried under the road surface & when a car equipped with another coil passes over it; it induces a current in the car's coil. This feeds into the EV's battery & keeps it topped up. Their research indicates that if 250 metres of every kilometre of motorway was fitted with wireless charging, an EV could travel along the motorway without depleting its reserves.

It is likely that some form of this wireless charging will be the future for charging EV's as it is convenient & people love convenience. It will also keep people away from dangerous electric currents & do away with the confusing cabling arrangements that currently exist.

# The charging network

It is fine looking at the future of EV charging, but what is important is the here & now. Currently, the charging networks around the world are somewhat sporadic, therefore the current situation in various countries are listed below.

## UK

On the 25$^{th}$ March 2019, Zapmap reported that the total number of public charging point locations in the UK to be 7,141 with the total number of connectors being 20,408. This is far less than the number of EV's on the road in the UK. It should therefore be clear that there are currently not enough charging points available to charge even 10% of the EV's in the UK.

Of those public charge points that are available in the UK, almost all are owned or operated by private companies. Currently there are around 20 large companies that operate chargers within the UK, but there are numerous other EV chargers available which are independently installed & run by smaller companies which may be available to users of larger networks, or just at the discretion of their owners.

In the UK, the EV charger networks are typically run by energy firms &/or other companies that want a slice of the pie from the growing car charging market. Some of the charge points are even run by local authorities & others by organisations who just wish to appear environmentally conscious.

All these companies vying for your custom sounds like fantastic news for any EV owner who is looking for somewhere to charge up, but every network is different & they each have different parameters.

For instance, the majority require the EV driver to pre-register & carry either a RFID card or to use a smart phone app, therefore the more networks you use, the more cards you will need to carry. Collectively they have vastly different membership models too; some operate a 'pay as you go' system, whilst some have hefty subscription fees, but some offer free power & minimal sign-up fees.

This energy network Wild West has all been created because of the UK government's policy that an operator will only be eligible for subsidies if they collect detailed data on their network users & their usage. As the government did not specify a standard method for data harvesting or network requirements, each of these companies created their own unique system, which ultimately is not user friendly. Clearly anyone repeatedly using their local network will be unaffected by the numerous requirements imposed by multiple companies, but if an EV driver wishes to drive across the country, through different networks, then it is important to check beforehand which operators will be potential sources of electricity for the traveller & the availability of charge points that will be available en-route. It would also be advisable to join the required networks in advance & allow plenty of time for any RFID cards to be posted.

Some of the smart phone apps require your credit or debit card info, then charge you based on the time & the power used. Most of the charge points are networked & the network tells the power point when to start & stop. Some of these apps ask you to pre-load money into your account, just as you would do with an Oyster card, allowing the EV driver to swipe before receiving any electricity. Tesla supercharger users pay either per kWh for the electricity supplied, or per minute spent whilst charging at the station.

One point to note is that red Tesla charge points are currently only available to Tesla owners, so it is not possible to use their red network if you do not own a Tesla EV.

There are a number of websites available that detail where these public chargers are located. These websites may not be 100% accurate as many rely on users to input the data, therefore it would be advisable to double check with numerous sites before opting to use a charge point if you are not familiar with it. In the UK, Googling 'zap map' or 'open charge' will point you to two of these such websites.

The main companies that operate chargers in the UK are: Alfapower, Alfen, Allego BV, Blink Network/ECOtality, Charge & Drive, Charge your car, Chargemaster, ChargeNow, Chargeplace Scotland, E-Car, Ecotricity, Elektrobay (UK), Elektromotive (UK), Engenie, EO Charging, ESB Ecars, Essent (NL), EV-Box, evcharge.online, Incharge, Innology SE (RWE eMobility), InstaVolt Ltd, Lidl, Nissan UK, Nomadpower, Plugged in Midlands (UK), POD Point (UK), POLAR (UK), RWE/Npower, Source London, Swarco E.Connect, Tesla Motors, The GeniePoint Network, The New Motion (NL), ubitricity & Zero Carbon World. All these can be found on the internet.

## EEC

The EEC have been busy preparing the way for EV charging by making various plans, partnerships & initiatives which has had mixed results. A country by country brief for the EEC is as follows (figures correct at time of print):

Austria has 2381 charging points in 906 locations. Czech Republic has 527 charging stations in 420 locations. Belgium 1,613 charging stations in 854 locations, Denmark has 824 charging stations in 365 locations. Estonia has 165 charging stations in 153 locations. Finland has 971 charging stations in 344 locations. France has 3,609 charging stations in 2,115 locations. Germany has 29,284 charging stations in 11,979 locations. Greece has 71 charging stations in 61 locations. Italy has 8,598 charging stations in 4,195 locations. Ireland has 1,231 charging stations in 648 locations.

Netherlands has 10,669 charging stations in 7,793 locations. Norway has 9,491 charging stations in 2,094 locations. Poland has 397 charging stations in 182 locations. Portugal has 1,373 charging stations in 657 locations. Slovenia has 140 charging stations in 96 locations. Spain has 2,412 charging stations in 1,443 locations. Sweden has 6,108 charging stations in 1,680 locations. Switzerland has 1,343 charging stations in 707 locations.

The overall network within the EEC is planned to increase to 2 million by 2025. Some of these countries have more charging stations than others, which equates to 76% of all EEC charging points being in just four countries (Netherlands, Germany, France & UK), whilst the country with the densest charging network is in the Netherlands.

There are at least three international charging networks that will allow charging in various EEC countries. They are: Plug Surfing, New Motion & Chargemap.

## Canada

Canada currently has 5,018 charging stations in 3,348 locations. In 2012, free public EV charging stations were installed along the main route of the Trans-Canada Highway by Sun Country Highway. As of 2012 it was the longest EV ready highway in the world.

The companies that operate chargers in Canada are: AeroVironment, Azra Network, BeCharged, Blink Network/ECOtality, ChargePoint (Coulomb Technologies), Circuit Electrique, Clipper Creek, EATON, flo, GE WattStation, GreenLots, SemaCharge Network, Sun Country Highway & Tesla Motors.

## USA

The USA currently has 33,530 charging stations in 21,389 locations. The companies that operate chargers in the USA are: AeroVironment, AVCON, BeCharged, Blink Network/ECOtality, ChargePoint (Coulomb Technologies), Clipper Creek, EATON, Electrify America, eVgo Network, EVite (ch), EVSE LLC WebNet, GE WattStation, GreenLots, MANGE Charge, Nissan, NRG EVgo, OpConnect, Plug-In North Central Washington, RCS (Revitalize Charging Solutions), SemaCharge Network, Shorepower, Sun Country Highway, Tesla Motors, Volta Charging & Westar Energy ElectroGo.

## South America

Argentina has 2 charging stations in 1 location. Brazil has 9 charging stations in 8 locations. Chile has 8 charging stations in 7 locations. Colombia has 35 charging stations in 7 locations & Ecuador has 2 charging stations in 2 locations.

## Australia

Australia currently has 389 charging stations in 160 locations. The companies that operate chargers in Australia are: Blink Network/ECOtality, ChargePoint (Coulomb Technologies), Chargestar (au), GreenLots, POD Point (UK), Queensland Electric Super Highway, RAC Electric Highway/ChargeStar, Stadtwerke Clausthal-Zellerfield, Tesla Motors & The REV Project (UWA – Australia).

## New Zealand

New Zealand currently has 908 charging stations in 512 locations. The companies that operate chargers within New Zealand are: charge.net.nz, chargeNET (lk), ChargeNow, ChargePoint (Coulomb Technologies), EV-Box, EVSE LLC Webnet, JuicePoint, Tesla Motors, Vector (NZ) & WEL Network (NZ).

## Japan

Japan has 1,529 charging stations in 1506 locations. The companies that operate chargers in Japan are: Stadtwerke Clausthal-Zellerfield & Tesla Motors.

## China

China has 1,732 charging stations in 384 locations. The company that operate the chargers in China are: Tesla Motors.

## Singapore

Singapore currently has 9 charging stations in 9 locations. The companies that operate chargers in Singapore are: GreenLots & Stadtwerke Clausthal-Zellerfield.

The majority of these network operators in these countries propose to expand the number of charging stations over the coming years, but some of these operators will disappear & others may take their place. However, it will be a sure bet that the number of chargers will slowly increase making EV ownership far easier.

# Chapter 7 – **Hidden costs**

There are some hidden costs associated with running an EV. Some may be obvious after reading this far, but some will not. For instance, to begin, the situation regarding insurance should be looked at.

## Insurance costs

In the UK, EV's face higher rates on insurance. This is partly due to the fact that the insurance companies claim that EV's are more expensive to repair as they contain "specialist parts" & need "specialist skills" to repair them. Currently in the UK, only 1% of the mechanics are qualified to work on the high-voltage electric systems on behalf of franchised dealerships. As a result of these factors, the insurance companies have increased the premiums & inflated the insurance grouping for EV's to group 22, which means they are all now in an expensive insurance category. This group is in the sport car range, which may be the result of Elon Musk at Tesla boasting about the sporty nature of their EV's & the impressive 0 – 60 speeds. For instance, their Roadster accelerates quicker than an F1 car. It gets from 0 – 60mph (0 – 100kph) in 1.9 seconds & can cover quarter of a mile in just 8.9 seconds. Modern F1 cars accelerate 0 – 60mph (0 – 100kph) between 2.1 – 2.7 seconds.

However, there is another factor that adds to the already inflated insurance cost. That is 'insurance premium tax' (IPT). This is where the government receives 12% of the premium paid as tax. The government could therefore reduce the cost of EV insurance instantly by reducing or removing the tax on the insurance, but they are unlikely to change this policy unless they are publically shamed or forced to do so.

As an example, the following insurance costs are based on GoCompare's average for a used car being insured by a 35 year old accountant living in Bristol who has a five year no claims discount. A Nissan Micra would cost the man £253 to insure, whilst a Nissan LEAF would cost £368. A Renault Clio would cost him £247 to insure, whilst a Renault Zoe would be a whopping £395. A sporty Volkswagen Golf GTI would cost the accountant £387, whilst the standard Volkswagen E-Golf would be £388. All these EV's are the electric equivalents to their corresponding ICE vehicle.

The average difference is that an EV will cost up to 60% more to insure than its ICE equivalent. In addition, there will be certain things that will not be covered on the insurance policy, such as the electrical cables that are needed to charge the EV. Therefore if one is damaged, vandalised or stolen when you leave your car charging in a public place, you may not be able to claim on the insurance. Public liability insurance will not be covered as standard too & this will be something that you will definitely need as a member of the public may trip over your cable whilst you are charging in a public place. It is therefore imperative that you have adequate public liability insurance as a standard EV insurance policy will purposely omit this. Also, as some EV's are available where the battery is leased to the purchaser of the vehicle, a separate insurance policy may be needed just to cover the battery.

The Nissan LEAF has an option where you can buy the car, but rent the battery from them. Also, Renault has up to now only leased their batteries. Therefore if you were to buy a second hand Renault EV, then you would not be buying the battery, just the car. Therefore it could be the case that two or more expensive insurance policies may be needed, rather than just one for an ICE powered vehicle.

It is not only the UK where this is the case, In the USA it is a similar story, but not quite as expensive.

An average man in California could expect to insure his ICE powered Fiat 500 for $1,597 & the equivalent electric model for $2,016. Therefore this is a 26% increase for the EV. An ICE powered Smart Fortwo could be insured for $1,474, whilst the electric model would cost $1,807. This is another hefty rise. This time an increase for the EV of 23% over the ICE.

## Battery lease

It could be an option to lease the battery for the EV rather than buy it outright. If this is an option, then you can expect to pay either a monthly or annual fee, a similar fee plus the mileage or for just the mileage. It will depend entirely on the lease agreement.

For instance, as a guide, you could expect to pay £59 per month for a 22kWh Renault Zoe battery that drives 6,000 miles per year. Any mileage over this level will be charged at an extra £0.08p per mile. With a Renault Zoe ZE40 battery that drives 6,000 miles per year, you could be paying £69 per month plus an extra £0.08p per mile if you drive more than 6,000 miles.

With Nissan, if you rent the battery on a 24kWh or 30kWh battery in a Nissan LEAF that drives 9,000 miles per year, with a 12 months rental agreement, then you would expect to pay £97 per month, plus an extra £0.075p per mile if you drive more than 9,000 miles.

Given the difference in the cost of the car with buying outright or buying the car & renting the battery, you could expect to save approximately £5,500 from the purchase price. If you look at the battery rental, it would have a pay-back period of approximately 5 years. Unfortunately, after this time, there is the ongoing rental cost, but with all these schemes, you have a guarantee on the level of the state of charge (SOC) that the battery can hold.

The SOC is the percentage of charge that the battery can hold. As batteries age, their SOC reduces. Therefore the performance of an old battery will fall below that of a new battery. When a battery falls below a certain threshold, it will be unusable & will need to be replaced. Most guarantee their batteries at either 75% or 60%, so if degradation falls below the level they specify, then they will replace the battery. If the car & battery was owned outright, then the owner would need to pay for the battery replacement costs.

The whole concept for the battery leasing was designed back when the EV manufacturers were bringing out their first EV models. The lease scheme was designed to alleviate the worry originating from the horror stories of battery deaths occurring from poor battery maintenance. It was a way of introducing useable EV's in to the marketplace, whilst offering peace of mind for the batteries. It is not clear if it worked, but second hand EV's that have hire agreements on their batteries command higher prices than those which are owned outright. This is because when the battery depreciates, so too does the value of the vehicle. Therefore, the older the EV, the more attractive it will be in the second hand market when compared to an identical one that was bought outright.

The battery lease arrangement offered by Nissan & Renault is with RCI Financial Services & part of their small print states that the vehicle & battery can not be exported to the following countries: Andorra, Austria, Belgium, France, Germany, Ireland, Italy, Liechtenstein, Luxemburg, Monaco, The Netherlands, Poland, Portugal, San Marino Slovenia, Spain, Sweden & Switzerland. Therefore selling the EV on the international market may prove problematic.

It would be possible to buy the lease for the battery, but the cost would be dependant on the age of the battery & the condition of it. If the battery had just been replaced, then obviously RCI would wish to recover their costs for the new battery.

Also, due to the nature of batteries degrading over time, **NEVER** buy a second hand EV, or sign a battery rental agreement without first physically checking the SOC & condition of the battery.

## Public charging

It was explained in the previous chapter that there are costs associated with charging EV's. Here the costs are examined. Firstly, as was previously stated, approximately 80% of charging an EV happens at home. Therefore it would make sense to have a dedicated charger installed there. This is because charging the EV uses a lot of electricity & a typical domestic socket was never designed to cope with this high level of electrical demand. Therefore, ideally a dedicated circuit will need to be installed directly from the circuit breaker.

This circuit will be similar to the one that may already be installed if you have an electric oven in your home & due to the dangerous nature of electrical wiring, **NEVER** attempt to install a circuit yourself unless you are qualified to do so or you may run the risk of electrocution, cause an electrical fire or at best invalidate your home insurance. The installation should therefore only be undertaken by a qualified individual who is able to guarantee their work. As with all things, some are cheaper than others. The higher the charge that the charger can deliver, the thicker the cabling that is needed, the circuit breaker will also need to handle more current & both these elements will add to the cost, therefore if your vehicle can only accept a maximum 7kW, then it is not worth paying for a 22kW unit. You may think that you are future-proofing your home, but in the future, when you change your vehicle, the current charge methods may have been superseded with a different system that is much faster.

In the UK there are numerous companies that will install a home charger. Pod-Point currently charge £779 for a 3.6kW charger, £859 for a 7kW charger & £1,499 for a 22kW charger. Although these costs can be currently be reduced by £500 if your installation meets the requirements for an EVHS grant. Most company's installations cost on average £1,000, but there are currently grants available to reduce the costs. In the UK, the energy saving trust is a good place to start when researching available grants.

The running costs on these home chargers can be calculated as follows. A 100kW Tesla Model S needs a charge of 100kW to fully charge from empty to full. But in the real world, it would need topping up, therefore it will be assumed the EV needs 80% (80% of 100kW is 80kW). If the electric costs £0.14.4p per kWh, then 80 x 0.14 = £11.20p to fully charge the vehicle overnight. If this charge was made overnight & an Economy 7 tariff was used, then this would cost £0.105p per kWh. To charge the same car from 20% to 100% overnight would cost 80 x 0.105 = £8.40p. The exact cost will differ from this as it will depend on the size of battery in your EV & the cost of electricity available to you on your tariff. It would therefore be advisable to find the tariff that best suits your needs to reduce the cost of the electricity.

Charging at work may also be an option. The average cost of installing a commercial charge point is in the region of £1,000 - £1,500 & grants are also currently available up to £500 for each charger up to a total of 20. These commercial chargers may make fiscal sense for a company to install as they will keep the profits from the mark-up in the cost of electricity sold to the persons using these chargers. These installations are designed to offer a payback period to the business of between 3 – 5 years if they are used for the majority of the time.
Any EV user who wishes to charge away from home will need to use the public network of chargers. The current costs are as follows in the UK:

'Alfapower' currently has no membership fee & charges 25p/kWh using their app or RFID card.

'Allego' currently has credit card or debit card charging with the Shell recharge network. There is no current membership fee & it can be accessed via their app at a rate of 25p/kWh. 'Charge your car' are free charge points that have a £20 membership fee for their RFID card. Although the electricity is free, they charge a flat rate £1 connection fee.

'Chargemaster' runs the POLAR network & operate two schemes. 'Polar Plus' has a membership fee of £7.85 per month & gives some free charging points & some which cost 10.8p/kWh. 'Polar Instant' offers a pay as you go (PAYG) network where the costs are £1 per hour for 3kW, £1.50 per hour for 3.6kW, 7kW, 11kW & 22kW. They also have some rapid chargers & charge £6 for 30 minutes. Access to all points on the PAYG scheme also incur a £1.20 admin fee.

'ChargeNow' is a service operated by BMW & uses the 'Chargemaster network'. BMW offer 3 months free membership.

'Chargeplace Scotland' offer access to their network via a £20 annual RFID card & the cost of electricity is free.

'Ecotricity' network is called 'Electric Highway' & is installed on the UK motorway service stations. The membership fee is free to join, but a smartphone is required to control the chargers. The costs are 30p/kWh & 15p/kWh for Ecotricity customers. They also have rapid chargers at IKEA stores, but the cost can be offset with a £6 discount off in store purchases.

'Engenie EV' offers PAYG rapid chargers. Access is free via a contactless credit or debit card & costs are set at either 36p/kWh or £4 flat fee per charge.

'ESB Ecars' are predominantly in Ireland. It is free to join, but you must have one of their RFID cards to operate their chargers. All electricity is currently free.

'Genie Point' requires users to register for free if you are using a smartphone, or £9 if you require a RFID card. Costs are 30p/kWh for Type 2 chargers at 7kW & 22kW, plus a 50p connection charge. Rapid units are 30p/kWh with a £1 connection charge. Inside the M25 there is an increased connection charge which is £1.80.

'InstaVolt' uses a PAYG rapid charging network that has no membership fees. Just use a contactless credit or debit card to access the charge points. Costs are 35p/kWh.
'Plugged in Midlands' operate in the Midlands. Membership is £7.85 per month via a RFID card & electricity is either charged at 10.8/kWh or free to use.

'POD Point' is free to join & is accessed via a smart phone app or a RFID card. Some points are free, but some are PAYG.

'Source London' has four current schemes. Full membership is £4 a month & accessed via a smart phone app or with a RFID card. Costs are 9.5p per minute for 22kW & 3.6p per minute for 7kW & 3kW units. Their flexi plan costs a one off £10 fee & costs 11.9p per minute for 22kW & 5.9p per minute for 7kW & 3kW. The PAYG plan costs 14.3p per minute for 22kW & 7p per minute for 7kW & 3kW. Their legacy units are free to use to anyone who has a suitable RFID card.

'Tesla Motors' are a little confusing. If you have an older Tesla, the network is free to use. All their vehicles ordered before 15$^{th}$ January 2017 & delivered before 15$^{th}$ April 2017 came with free lifetime supercharging which will follow the vehicle. Tesla offered lifetime supercharging through its referral program until September 2018, but this was only available for the original purchaser of the car & therefore it does not transfer to any new owner. Tesla's Model S & Model X vehicles ordered from 15$^{th}$ April 2017 through to 2$^{nd}$ November 2018 include a 400 kWh of free annual supercharging credits, which are good for approximately 1,000 miles of driving.

Tesla has also offered free supercharging as part of its referral program. Those referral perks are non-transferrable. On 21st March 2019 Tesla reintroduced its referral program; the chief perk of which is 1,000 miles of free supercharging (about 400 kWh) for both the new car buyer & the referring owner. Apart from this, any Tesla ordered after 15th January 2017 will need to pay for their access to the supercharger network. A smart phone app or RFID card is required to access their network for the supercharger & destination chargers. The destination chargers are free to use, but parking charges may apply. If you have to pay for use of the supercharger, it is 27p/kWh.

'Ubitricity' offer lamp post charging in certain Boroughs in London. Tariffs & costs all vary dependant on location & the network is accessed via an ubitricity smart cable that plugs into the lamp post. Each cable is linked to an account. Other regions also have similar 'local networks'.

'Zero Carbon World' run PAYG charge points for the hospitality industry. They encourage their customers to offer free charges, but many are PAYG.

It is therefore impossible to quantify how much an EV will cost to charge per year as every EV driver will be in a different location, using a mixture of networks & tariffs. The situation is similar in every country where there is a choice of networks & tariffs.

If UK registered EV's are driven in the EEC, then charge points can be found on either the 'plug share' website or on the 'chargemap' website. There are at least three international networks that are useable in most of the EEC: 'Plug Surfing', 'New Motion', & 'chargemap', all of which offer access to chargers in several European countries. All these three offer access to a range of European operators using an RFID card, key fob or a smart phone app with payment made either with PayPal or a credit or debit card at the charge station. The most accessible chargers will be found in France, Germany, Belgium, Luxembourg & the Netherlands.

More specific country information can be found on both the RAC & AA websites.

## Private charging

Everyone with an EV will need to charge at home, this is usually something that is undertaken overnight in a garage. The UK government claim that 80% of all EV charging occurs at home, overnight.

As was previously seen, a charge point will need to be used to do this & after this has been installed, it will cost money to charge your EV. How much this cost will be is exactly like asking how long a piece of string is. This is all due to the many variables. Just how long will the vehicle actually be charging for, how much power will it be using when it is charging, how big is the battery, how much charge is required & how much does the electricity cost? All these variables will need to be known before an exact cost can be calculated accurately. So some assumptions will be made & here an overnight charge for a Nissan LEAF will be calculated as the LEAF is an average EV & therefore will be applicable to the most individuals.

The average cost of electricity in the UK is 14.4p per kWh & if a 3kWh charger was used to charge the 40kWh Nissan LEAF overnight (13.3 hours) to fully charge the EV, a range of 166 miles would cost £5.76. If a 7kW charger was used, the time spent charging would reduce, but not the amount of electricity. To charge a 40kWh LEAF overnight (5.7 hours). The figure often quoted for ICE powered vehicles is that they generally cost 12p per mile to run & over an estimated annual 9,000 miles with an average 45mpg, running an ICE would cost £1,209 in fuel with the cost to a 40kWh EV being £300, so the EV would cost approximately 75% less in fuel. However, a small percentage will need to be added to the £300 for the cost of the charge point & the cost of charging cables as they will also factor into the costs.

# Environmental costs

Everything has an impact on the environment. Ever since mankind moved from being hunter gathers to farming there was a heavy cost on the environment. When mankind subsequently moved from farming to urbanisation, that cost increased again. When industrialisation & mechanisation became the norm, the cost increased sevenfold. EV's have therefore been hailed as having 'green credentials' & bucking the trend, but nothing could be further from the truth.

## Carbon credits

It was already seen in chapter 2, the International Energy Agency (IEA) reported that in 2016, 65.3% of the world's electricity was obtained by burning fossil fuels. This will have a cost on the environment. Especially as the companies who create electricity in this manner purchase 'carbon credits' which basically allows them to pollute without having any government or organisation being able to point a finger at them. One carbon credit allows a company to produce 1 tonne of carbon dioxide or the equivalent amount of other greenhouse gases. There are even markets where these carbon credits can be bought or sold. They are just a licence to allow companies to pollute, but as governments are allowed to issue/sell x amount per year under the Kyoto Protocol, every government is allowed to issue these polluting licences to whomever they wish. They are then sold to the highest bidder on the open market. Whether a company buys these licences that allow them to pollute, or not. They still pollute. It is not a magic piece of paper that will magic the pollution away, it just magic's away the negative publicity.

With regard to the EV market, there is a large number of polluting elements that go into each vehicle. Even when the plastics that are used in them which are all produced from petrochemicals are ignored.

Nickel, lithium & cobalt are used in the EV batteries & the mining & refining process's for these elements are one of the most polluting processes on the planet. Only the companies who mine these elements are set to see benefits, not the environment.

## Nickel

Nickel is the fifth most common element on the planet. It is not only used in batteries, but also in anything made with stainless steel &/or electronics. The annual growth in nickel use is growing by 4% every year. The majority of nickel comes from mines in Australia, Canada, Indonesia, Russia & the Philippines. Nickel is derived from sulphide ores & laterite ores. Sulphide ores are usually mined from underground mines, whilst the laterite ore is generally obtained by open pit mining. Then begins the extractive metallurgy, which is very similar to the way crude oil is reduced down to various products. Here, the ore is crushed & heated repeatedly until elements can be removed & smelted.

Due to the emissions of carbon dioxide & sulphur dioxide during the mining & refining process, nickel is ranked as the 8th most polluting of 63 metals with regard to its potential for global warming. It is so toxic that it is not currently recycled from batteries. Recycling nickel is seen as being far too dangerous. An effective recycling system would therefore need to be established to reduce the effects of nickel. Issuing carbon credits will not make this metal any less toxic or any less damaging to the environment.

Also, there is always a serious environmental impact that occurs near factories that produce the nickel. In Russia there was a factory town called Norilsk where there was a nickel plant. The death rate there is four times the average of other Russian cities.

This town is not an isolated example, this always happens near nickel factories. If the use of nickel creates pollution that is allowed to spread into the global atmosphere, the human cost could be huge as nickel is a known carcinogenic metal.

## Cobalt

Cobalt is used in batteries & magnets. The extraction of cobalt is similar to that used for nickel. In fact it is generally a secondary element obtained in nickel or copper processing. Half of the world's cobalt originates in the Congo. 20% of it is produced by 'artisanal miners', which translates from propaganda speak to individuals working in terrible conditions by hand. According to 'The Carter Centre' it is estimated that half of the Congo's 'artisanal miners' are children who carry, crush & wash the raw ore for twelve hours a day for pennies. In 2012, it was estimated that there were 40,000 children working in these mines. Many large global companies are buying the cobalt that is obtained in this manner. As EV's will increase demand for cobalt, the situation is unlikely to resolve itself, but just get worse.

## Lithium

Lithium is a vital component in modern EV batteries. Between 80 – 90% of all lithium originates in Australia & South America (Argentina, Bolivia & Chile which has 54% of the world's lithium). Due to an increase in demand for lithium, extraction from the ore has moved from that detailed with nickel to a water based process. This is where large shallow reservoirs are dug, then filled with water & then crushed ore. When the water evaporates, mineral salts are left which can then be removed & filtered to remove the lithium along with many other elements.

It is twice as cost effective as nickel processing & produces less carbon emissions, but the amount of water used removes it from the immediate environment, which leaves the vegetation, animals & indigenous humans without a source of water. It takes one & a half million gallons of water to produce one tonne of lithium.

High use in batteries is pushing the demand for lithium. As the water evaporation is a slow process, partly processed material is now being shipped to China for processing & this transport cost is estimated to use three times more energy than seen in the nickel process. Additionally, it is estimated that only 5% of lithium-ion batteries ever get recycled, therefore 11 million tonnes of lithium-ion batteries could find their way into landfill by 2030 rather than being recycled. It should therefore be clear that an EV will pollute the environment. It may not pollute the immediate area around it like an ICE vehicle, but the pollution it produces will be caused elsewhere. It will be just as real & just as damaging, but how much?

## $CO_2$ emissions

Much research has gone into answering the question as to which costs more to the environment, an ICE powered vehicle or an EV. With regard to production costs, an EV is the same as an ICE powered vehicle, but when the battery is factored in, the production of the EV is far more harmful to the environment as the energy that has gone into the production produces far more $CO_2$.

However, this is for a new car, but they do not stay 'new' for long as they are driven. Therefore it is important to know how much $CO_2$ is produced by an average ICE vehicle & an average EV, but as was seen earlier, the composition of each countries electricity is made from different things & different proportions; therefore each countries electricity has a different level of $CO_2$.

An average ICE powered vehicle would use approximately 300g $CO_2$/km, with a hybrid being in the range of 180g $CO_2$/km after including manufacturing, fuel combustion & fuel production.

Paraguay produces a large proportion of its electricity using hydro-electricity (electricity made by water driven turbines) so their EV's would produce an estimated 70g $CO_2$/km. India produces the majority of its electricity from burning coal, so their EV's would produce an estimated 370g $CO_2$/km, which is far worse than the ICE vehicle. China's EV's are in the region of 258g $CO_2$/km, USA is approximately 202g $CO_2$/km (average as it varies from state to state). The UK is in the range of 189g $CO_2$/km & in Canada, it is approximately 115g $CO_2$/km. The electricity in France works out to be approximately 93g $CO_2$/km as they generate a large proportion of their electricity from nuclear, so their cars are powered by greener electricity than the UK. Iceland electricity is greener still as they produce a lot of electricity from geothermal power. Their electricity has an estimated cost of 70g $CO_2$/km.

It therefore depends on exactly where you live before you can estimate what the electricity that you use to power your EV actually costs the environment, but it should be obvious that it would be far better for the environment to drive an ICE powered vehicle in India, but an EV in Iceland or France.

## Health costs

There is a known risk with all EV's, but the majority of the research has all been undertaken by the EV industry directly, or they have funded the studies. None of this 'research' can therefore be said to be impartial & at best it can be compared to the tobacco industry who undertook research so as to sidestep any publically funded research.

However, there has been some impartial research undertaken & those results have had the opposite results to those published or paid for by the EV manufacturers. Therefore, until there is more impartial research undertaken by impartial sources, any stories read online or on the news should be treated with scepticism.

## Electromagnetic radiation

There is a possibility that hybrid &/or electric cars may be cancer causing as they emit extremely low frequency (ELF) electromagnetic fields (EMF). If this turns out to be true, then there is a real risk to any or all occupants in an EV.
Peer reviewed laboratory studies that have been conducted over several decades have found that biologic effects from limited exposures to ELF & EMF. EMF has detrimental effects on humans, but the recognised guidelines are set by the self appointed , International Commission on Non-Ionizing Radiation Protection (ICNIRP) & the studies have found that these 'guidelines' are inadequate when it comes to protecting health.

At present, more than 230 EMF experts have signed the 'International EMF Scientist Appeal' (IEMFSA) which calls on the 'World Health Organisation' to create stronger guidelines for ELF & radio frequency EMF. This is IEMFSA is actually in line with findings published by the 'International Agency for Research on Cancer of the World Health Organisation, who stated in 2001 that magnetic fields have been considered 'possibly carcinogenic' in humans. They go on to recommend that all consumer products should therefore be shielded from EMF. This would be particularly important in EV's as the driver & passengers could potentially spend a lot of time exposed to these EMF's.

Even a traditional ICE powered car with driving aids will produce levels that humans can not tolerate for a long period according to Theodore P. Metsis, Ph.D., who is an electrical, mechanical & environmental engineer from Athens, Greece. These driver aids include, but are not limited to ABS, tire pressure sensors, IR pedestrian warning systems, front object laser detection, night time pedestrian warning system, night vision, lane departure system, rear CCD, slide curtain sensor, blind spot detection, rear object laser, airbags, airbag sensors, collision sensors, some types of cruse control & wheel speed sensors.

The occupants of the EV are also exposed to the EMF from the electrical wiring embedded in the vehicle & also from the magnets. One impartial study tested a Renault Megane diesel & a Renault ZOE 42kW together, on the same roads at the same time over a range of conditions. The results were interesting as the International Agency for Research on Cancer (IARC) states that any extended exposure to EMF's stronger than 200 nanoTesla to be a 'possible cause' for cancer. The maximum level recorded in the ZOE's driver seat was 4,389 nanoTesla whilst the maximum level in the Megane was 2,889 nanoTesla. Therefore it can be seen that driving a ZOE exposes the driver to a far higher level of EMF than he/she would experience driving a diesel vehicle.

Any increased exposure to an EMF could ultimately increase the risks associated with cancer, therefore unless EV's are made with built in shielding, it is probable that there will be an increase in cancer rates throughout the developed world.
It should be noted that if the risks associated with EMF's in EV's are just fiction, why does the UK Government give guidance to MOT testers (an MOT is an annual test to ensure that a vehicle is safe to drive on the road) that anyone who has a pacemaker fitted should not be in the vicinity of an EV or hybrid due to the presence of an EMF. EMF's interfere with the operation of pacemakers, therefore there is a risk, or they would not issue such advice.

## Particulate matter

ICE vehicles, especially diesels are said to produce a high proportion of 'particulate matter' (PM), which are small particles that originate from vehicles that are less than 5% the thickness of a human hair. This PM also originates from EV's, but this is not usually acknowledged in any statistics, but is a fact, so this clearly demonstrates the fact that you can never trust governmental or NGO statistics.

The tyres & brakes of any vehicle produce PM. If it is diesel, petrol, electric or anything else, even bicycles produce PM. It is estimated that 18% of PM has originated from ICE exhausts, which is why governments & city councils are wanting to ban ICE vehicles from cities & eventually from the countryside too, but 11% of PM originates from brakes & tyres, so it would appear that banning ICE vehicles & using EV's will only reduce PM emissions, not remove it, but this fact is not publicised. It is ignored by politicians, policy makers, the media & those who are blindly pushing to 'green' the world.

## Pedestrian casualties

As EV's do not use an ICE & hybrids do not use their ICE at low speeds, they are very quiet. Just the noise from the rolling resistance of the tyres on the ground can be heard, so many accidents have occurred in urban areas with pedestrians. This is due to the fact that everyone has grown up to the sound of the ICE & is therefore aware of the sound subconsciously. The sound of rubber on tarmac is not yet embedded into the human psyche so people do not act 'automatically' to the sound & when an EV is travelling less than 12mph (20kph), the sound is hardly audible at all, especially amongst the noise of a city.

This has an effect on cyclists, blind people as well as deaf & the hard of hearing. Because of this, EV's & hybrids are 37% more likely to hit a pedestrian than an ICE powered vehicle & 57% more likely to hit a cyclist.

To combat this, governments around the world have began to create legislation that will ensure that all EV's & hybrids will produce audible noises. From July 2019, all new EV & hybrid models that are to seek approval in Europe will have to emit a noise when travelling at low speeds as outlined in an EU directive. In addition, in the EEC, by 2021, all EV's & hybrids must have a noise emitter fitted. Tesla, Volkswagen & BMW have all said they will wait for the legislation to be enacted before they fit any audio warnings to their vehicles.

Japan & the USA have all independently issued legislation to ensure that slow moving EV's & hybrids will issue warning sounds in the near future.

### Fire

The risk of fire & chemical burns will always be a risk with EV's & hybrids due to the volatile nature of the batteries that are contained within them. The most common battery chemistry used in EV's & hybrids is currently Li-Ion, & these batteries will spontaneously & violently combust if their contents came into contact with water, or even to the air as they also react violently in normal atmospheric conditions because of its spontaneous reaction with oxygen. They will even spontaneously combust if they reach a temperature of 65°C.

Li-Ion batteries therefore contain a highly volatile element which could cause problems if they were ever to malfunction, or were to become damaged due to a traffic accident. Li-Ion batteries are even not recommended to be used in situations where they are vibrated, so even a bumpy road could cause a fire in a Li-Ion battery. Even the electrolyte (lithium hexafluorophosphate) is highly flammable & has the potential to ignite things in close proximity. This electrolyte can also cause severe chemical burns & is toxic to humans, plants & animals.

If an EV is involved in a road traffic accident, the crash scene would need to be decontaminated by the emergency services. This is all due to the fact that any combustion gasses will be toxic & also any liquids spilt or leaking will be toxic & harmful as well as being highly combustible chemicals. It may therefore be advisable to carry foam, $CO_2$ or a powdered graphite extinguisher in the EV at all times. If the Lithium in the battery actually catches fire, use a Class D fire extinguisher.

## Electrocution

The risk of electrocution from an EV is a very real danger if any of the electric circuits are damaged or if they are malfunctioning. Advice to mechanics who work on vehicles is to stand on a thick rubber mat to avoid electrocution. In the even of electrocution occurring, garages are advised to use a long rubber coated hook to drag the mechanic away from the offending vehicle & therefore away from the source of electric.

These are safety measures for trained professionals; therefore it should impress upon you the fact that it is imperative to always allow trained professionals to undertake any repairs on an EV. **NEVER** attempt any work yourself.

## The taxpayer

Throughout the world there are incentives offered by various governments that will pay a certain amount or percentage when an individual purchases an EV or a home charger. They will also pay towards the installation of public chargers. But these subsidies & incentives are paid for by the taxpayers, but do the taxpayers benefit?

Currently EV's are not cheap. They are generally priced in the upper range, therefore it would be safe to assume that the majority of the EV buyers are higher earners who can afford to pay the higher costs associated with EV ownership. Those on the lower run of the ladder must make do with cheap vehicles from the second hand market. There are not many EV's making it into this lower portion of the market.

Therefore all the government incentives which refund a cash amount when you purchase a new EV, or receive a rebate for a home charger for an EV will be paid for from the governments coffers, just like when a company is paid for installing a public charger. But in each of these cases, it only benefits those who can afford an EV. Which are those who are at the top.

Electricity prices & taxes are increasing to pay for this EV network, but those who pay the smallest percentage from their earnings receive all the rewards. This may be a perverse system that imposes taxes on every member of a society, then gives a refund to those at the top, but that is the system that is currently being used build up the EV network globally.
Many on the lowest runs of the ladder do not even have an outside space where they could charge an EV, even if they wanted to. Life is never fair!

# Chapter 8 – **Grants & initiatives**

As was touched on in the last chapter, around the world there are currently various grants & initiatives that are available to purchasers of EV's. These are mainly made up of purchase rebates, tax exemptions & tax credits & other perks which can range from bus lane access to fee waivers on charging, parking & tolls.

An overview on some of these are listed below.

## UK

In the UK, the Plug-in Car Grant started on 1$^{st}$ January 2011. This covered EV's & PHEV's, but as of 21$^{st}$ October 2018, the grant was changed. Hybrids were excluded from the grant & the EV rebate was reduced from £4,500 down to £3,500 (this started at £5,000), so today, EV's are £1,500 more expensive & hybrids are £2,500 more expensive. They have also announced that they will ban sales of all new petrol & diesel ICE vehicles by 2040 & Scotland has proposed a ban on the same vehicles by 2032.

The UK government categorise EV's & hybrids into 3 distinct categories.

### Category 1 vehicles

These are EV's with a range of 70 miles making zero emissions & a manufacturer quoted $CO_2$ emissions figure of less than 50g/km which have been approved by the UK government are eligible for the grant.

## Category 1 cars

Vehicles that are in this category are: Audi e-tron, BMW i3 & i3s, BYD e6, Citroen CZero, Hyundai IONIQ Electric, Hyundai KONA Electric, Hyundai NEXO, Jaguar I-PACE, Kia e-Niro, Kia Soul EV, Mercedes-Benz B-Class Electric Drive, Nissan e-NV200 (5-seater & 7-seater), Nissan LEAF, Peugeot iON, Renault ZOE, Smart EQ Fortwo, Smart EQ Forfour, Tesla Model S, Tesla Model X, Toyota Mirai, Volkswagen e-up! & the Volkswagen e-Golf.

Each of these vehicles listed fall in to this category (correct as of date of publication[15]) & benefit from the grant which pays 35% of the cars value, up to a maximum amount of £3,500.

## Category 1 vans

Vans are also included. Electric vans must have $CO_2$ emissions of less than 75g/km, travel at least 10 miles (16km) between charges & have been approved by the UK government to be eligible for the grant. They are: BD Otomotiv eTraffic, BD Otomotiv eDucato, Citroen Berlingo, Mitsubishi Outlander Commercial, Nissan e-NV200 (cargo van), Peugeot ePartner, Renault Kangoo ZE, Renault Master ZE, LDV EV80 van & LDV EV80 chassis cab.

The van grant will pay for 20% of the purchase price up to a maximum of £8,000.

---

[15] https://www.gov.uk/plug-in-car-van-grants - 19/04/2019

## Category 1 motorbikes

Also, motorbikes that produce no $CO_2$ emissions, can travel at least 31 miles (50km) between charges & have been approved by the UK government are eligible for the grant. They are currently: Askoll eS3, Askoll eSpro 70, BMW C evolution, Eccity 125, Eccity 125+, Energica Ego, Energica Eva, Scutum Silence S02, Torrot Muvi, Vmoto 100, Vmoto 120 & Zero Motorcycles (all models).

Each of these motorbikes listed fall in to this category & benefit from a grant which pays 20% of the purchase price, up to a maximum of £1,500.

## Category 1 mopeds

Mopeds are included too & these need to produce no $CO_2$ emissions, travel at least 19 miles (30km) between charges & have been approved by the UK government to be eligible for the grant. They are currently: Askoll eS1, Askoll eS2, Askoll eSpro 45, GOVECS GO! T, NIU M-Series, NIU M+, NIU N-Series, NIU NGT, NIU U-Series, Torrot Muvi City, UGBEST e-City, Vespa Elettrica, Vmoto Super Soco CUX, Vmoto Super Soco TC & Vmoto Super Soco TS1200R.

These mopeds listed fall in to this category & benefit from a grant which pays 20% of the purchase price, up to a maximum of £1,500.

## Category 1 taxis

Taxis are also included & a taxi must produce $CO_2$ emissions of less than 50g/km, travel at least 70 miles (112km) without producing any emissions. Only one taxi is currently approved & that is LEVC TX. This taxi is eligible for a grant for 20% of the purchase price up to a maximum of £7,500.

## Category 2 vehicles

These are vehicles with a range of at least 10 miles whilst producing zero emissions & have a manufacturer quoted $CO_2$ emission figure of less than 50g/km.

These vehicles used to qualify for a 35% reduction if they cost under £60,000 with a maximum amount saved at £2,500. However, the 2018 reforms mean Category 2 vehicles no longer qualify for a grant, but are still eligible for a home charging point grant.

## Category 3 vehicles

These are vehicles with a range of at least 20 miles whilst producing zero emissions & have a manufacturer quoted $CO_2$ emission figure of between 50 - 75g/km.

These vehicles used to qualify for a 35% reduction if they cost under £60,000 with a maximum amount saved at £2,500. However, the 2018 reforms mean Category 3 vehicles no longer qualify for a grant, but are still eligible for a home charging point grant.

It is worth noting that, all the Category 1 vehicles are pure EV's, but if a PHEV could run with $CO_2$ emissions lower than 50g/km & was capable of travelling for 70 miles solely on electric power, it could also qualify for the grant. Unfortunately, that range for a PHEV is still a long way off & if it is ever achieved & actually meets the criteria for category 1 vehicles, the grant may have been reduced to zero.

EV buyers do not need to do anything to receive the grant as the dealer they are buying from will handle all the paperwork. The grant is just deducted from the cars list price. Used cars have never been eligible for the grant.

# Electric vehicle homecharge scheme (EVHS)

However, new & used cars are all eligible for an electric vehicle home charge grant, providing it is on the governments list of ultra-low emission vehicles that have been approved by the Office for Low Emission Vehicles.

These vehicles are those that are in category 1 cars, category 1 vans, category 1 motorbikes & category 1 mopeds.
In addition, the following category 2 cars are also included: Audi A3 e-tron, Audi Q7, BMW 225xe, BMW 330e, BMW 530e, BMW i8, Hyundai IONIQ PHEV, Kia Niro PHEV, Kia Optima PHEV, Mercedes-Benz C350 e (with 17 inch rear wheels), Mercedes-Benz E350 e SE, Mitsubishi Outlander PHEV (except Commercial), Toyota Prius Plug-in, Volkswagen Golf GTE, Volkswagen Passat GTE, Volvo S90 Twin Engine, Volvo V60 D5 Twin Engine, Volvo V60 D6 Twin Engine, Volvo V90 Twin Engine & Volvo XC60 Twin Engine.
Category 3 cars are also included & they are: Mercedes-Benz S500 Hybrid, Mercedes-Benz E350 e AMG Line, MINI Countryman PHEV, Porsche Panamera S E-Hybrid, Range Rover P400e & Range Rover Sport P400e.

All these vehicles are eligible for a grant from the Office for Low Emission Vehicles (OLEV) to install a home charger for their plug-in vehicle through the Electric Vehicle Homecharge Scheme. This provides a grant of up to 75% of the eligible costs for a charge point installation (up to £500, inc VAT) for the registered keeper, lessee or nominated primary user of a new or second hand eligible electric vehicle on or after 1st April 2015 onwards.

There is a range of requirements to be eligible for this grant which includes off street parking, proof of ownership to the land & the vehicle (or authorised user of the vehicle) & you must use one of the OLEV approved installers.

All the requirements for the EVHS & the EV grant could change at a moments notice as the schemes are run by government departments. Therefore it is important that you undertake your own research regarding obtaining grants to ensure you have the current & correct information before you make any purchases.

## Workplace charging schemes

Businesses, public sector organisations & charities that are registered in the UK can currently apply for an OLEV grant (called Workplace Charging Scheme (WCS)) that will provide up to 75% of the cost for a maximum of 20 charge points, which equates to £500 per socket (£10,000).

Eligible businesses just need to declare a need for charge points 'to encourage use by their staff, fleet, customers or the public'. The business must be located in England, Scotland, Wales or Northern Ireland & have dedicated off street parking. The property where they are to be located must also be owned by the business, or be able to provide written consent from the Landlord if the property is leased.

The business does not even need to have EV's, but if they do not, they must be able to provide evidence that they intend to purchase EV's, or encourage staff to take up EV's. If the business plans to charge customers for their use of these points, then the installation will not be eligible for WCS funding.

Standard UK three-pin sockets are not eligible for funding & the charge points can only be fitted by accredited OLEV installers. The points must provide a minimum of 3 kW & the supply must not be diminished when charging multiple vehicles simultaneously. Businesses cannot claim for existing charge points as the WCS grant is available only for new charge points that are yet to be installed.

The majority of these workplace installations opt for wall mounted charge points as they are typically cheaper to install. The alternative is a post, which are good, but usually have higher installation costs due to the need to route the cabling underground to the post.

For businesses who plan to install their charge points in locations which are accessible by the public are advised to install chargers that use RFID cards or fobs to stop any unwanted use by the public.

However, if your business is in the in the hotel, tourist or leisure industry, then it is possible that you could receive free charge point from 'Zero Carbon World'. If successful, then your business only has to pay for the installation costs.

## On street parking schemes

Because 40% of the UK population has no access to off-street parking, they have to park in the street. This has therefore been a sticking point which has been difficult to overcome when attempting to encourage individuals to buy EV's.

Therefore the government has set up the On-street Residential Chargepoint Scheme (OSRCS) which is designed to allow EV owners to apply to have a charge point installed on their street, even right outside their house, but the problem is that they have to apply through their local council.

If your Local Authority has already obtained funding & installed charge points, there is no guarantee that it will be available for you to use because any EV or hybrid driver will be able to use it. You will also have to pay to have access to the charge point. So it will be impossible to charge your EV overnight every day or even at all in some circumstances.

Anyone wishing to encourage their Local Authority to install charge points in their area should in the first instance contact their Local Authority.

The OSRCS was launched in 2016, but by January 2018 only Portsmouth City Council, Cambridge City Council, Luton Borough Council, Kettering Borough Council & The Royal Borough of Kensington & Chelsea had used the scheme to install charging points.

## London congestion charge exemption

The London Congestion Charge (LCC) was first introduced in February 2003 & there have been changes to the scheme over the years. Initially if a car produced less than 100g/km of $CO_2$, it was exempt from the charge. The current level is now set at 75g/km which is a level no ICE petrol or diesel cars can currently achieve. Therefore to be eligible for exemption from the LCC, you must drive an EV or hybrid as these are the only vehicles that can meet the 75g/km limit. The LCC operates between 7am & 6pm, every week day (Monday to Friday). It is not in operation out of these hours, on weekends or on bank holidays.

Between 8th April 2019 & 24th October 2021, the newer 75g/km standard will be in place for vehicles to qualify for the Cleaner Vehicle Discount (CVD). To achieve this, Vehicles must: meet the Euro 6 emission standard, emit no more than 75g/km & have a minimum 20 mile zero emission capable range.

Then from 25th October 2021 & 24th December 2025, only pure EV's will be eligible for the CVD. All other vehicles, regardless of their emissions will need to pay the congestion charge, unless they are registered for another discount or have an exemption.

As EV's are classed as zero emission vehicles, they are exempt from paying the London Congestion Charge which is currently set at £11.50 per weekday (once an initial £10 registration fee has been paid every year). They will therefore be fine until 24th December 2025. Hybrids that can meet the current standards will be exempt until 24th October 2021.

There is no automatic exemption. Each & every vehicle will need an application form filled in to apply for the exemption. If the vehicle is a UK registered PHEV, then the applicant will need to supply a photocopy of a conformity certificate as part of the application, along with a photo of the vehicles V5 document.

Non UK registered cars will need to supply a photograph of the vehicle registration document that was issued by the relevant overseas vehicle licensing agency. The document must clearly show that the vehicle meets the Euro 6 emission standard, emits no more than 75g/km & have a minimum 20 mile zero emission capable range. Alternatively, the registration document can clearly demonstrate that the vehicle is powered by electric.

The exemption will last one year & will therefore need to be renewed. The current cost is £10. If the vehicle does not have a current exemption certificate the current cost to drive in the zone is £11.50 per day, Monday – Friday.
The only other exemptions that are allowed are for those vehicles that are registered with the DVLA as one of the following:

Two-wheeled motorbikes (& sidecars) & mopeds, emergency service vehicles such as ambulances & fire engines which have a taxation class of 'ambulance' or 'fire engine' on the date of travel, NHS vehicles that are exempt from vehicle tax, vehicles used by disabled people that are exempt from vehicle tax & have a 'disabled' taxation class or vehicles for more than one disabled person that are exempt from vehicle tax & have a 'disabled' taxation class.

## London toxicity charge

There was also another charge called a 'Toxicity charge', or 'T-charge' which was introduced on 23$^{rd}$ October 2017 & operated in the same zone as the LCC & had the same hours of operation (7am to 6pm, Monday to Friday). It applied mainly to ICE diesel & ICE petrol vehicles which were registered before 2006, but also included later models.

The toxicity charge cost was an additional £10 a day for vehicles that were eligible to pay. It applied only to pre Euro 4 emission level vehicles. Therefore all hybrids, EV's & PHEV's were exempt from paying the fee.

The toxicity charge remained in place until 8$^{th}$ April 2019 when it morphed into the London ultra low emission zone.

## London ultra low emission zone exemption

Unlike the LCC which operates between Monday – Friday, the London ultra low emission zone (ULEZ) is the worlds first & is in operation 24 hours a day, 7 days a week, every day of the year within the same area of central London as the Congestion Charge. It is in addition to the LCC, so any vehicle that does not have an exemption will have to pay both the LCC & the ULEZ charges. The ULEZ clock starts at 12 midnight, so if you drive into the zone at 11pm & leave at 3am the next day, you will need to pay for two days.

The ULEZ will be phased in, starting on 8$^{th}$ April 2019 within the LCC zone. Then on 25$^{th}$ October 2021 it will be extended to the whole of London (South of the North Circular & North of the South Circular), which is 18 times bigger than the area covered by the first phase. Also, on 21$^{st}$ October 2020, any vehicle over 3.5 tonnes will be eligible to pay the ULEZ & the area covered will be from Enfield in the North to Croydon in the South. Hillingdon in the West to Havering in the East.

Any vehicle which does not meet the ULEZ standard will have to pay the charge. Cars, motorbikes, mopeds, vans & minibuses are currently set at £12.50 (on top of the LCC) whilst lorries (over 3.5 tonnes) & busses (over 5 tonnes) will face a charge currently set at £100 per day.

The current levels are set as follows: Euro 6 for ICE diesel cars, minibuses & vans. Therefore their engines must not produce more than 0.5g/km of carbon monoxide, 0.08g/km of nitrogen oxide or 0.005g/km of particulate matter.

Euro 4 for ICE petrol cars, minibuses & vans. Therefore their engines must not produce more than 1g/km of carbon monoxide or 0.08g/km of nitrogen oxide.

Euro 3 for ICE motorbikes, whose engines must not produce more than 2.3g/km of carbon monoxide & 0.15g/km of nitrogen oxide. HGV & busses will apply to those who do not meet Euro VI standards.

Any vehicle that falls outside the current level must pay the ULEZ fee. Therefore as a guide, it will generally affect diesel cars manufactured before 2015 & petrol cars manufactured before 2006. The vehicle registration document (V5) should identify a vehicle's Euro emission standard, but this is clearly another 'poor tax' imposed on those who can not afford to purchase a new vehicle which complies with these Euro emission standards.

All EV's are instantly compliant with the emission standards set for the ULEZ, but still have to pre-register for exemption otherwise they will be treated as having failed to pay & liable to a penalty which is currently set at £160 (which is reduced to £80 if paid within 14 days).

Hybrids should also be compliant with the emission standards set for the ULEZ, but will also have to pre-register for exemption otherwise they too will be treated as having failed to pay & liable to a penalty which is currently set at £160 (which is reduced to £80 if paid within 14 days).

## Road tax exemption

In the UK, road tax (which the government calls vehicle excise duty VED) is applicable to all vehicles. However, on 1st April 2017 the VED rules were changed. VED is now calculated on the $CO_2$ emissions on all vehicles registered since March 2001. Before that date, the VED is calculated from the size of the ICE.

EV's are classed as zero emission vehicles, therefore they are zero rated for the first & for all subsequent years, therefore the EV is does not pay any road tax so long as it does not fall into the 'premium rate' VED category.

PHEV's produce $CO_2$ emissions, therefore they are currently subject to VED. How much is dependant on the emissions. This could cost anything between £10 & £100 in the first year. Every subsequent year following that, will cost £140.
Premium rate vehicles apply to vehicles that cost £40,000 or more (including EV's). The VED for these vehicles are applicable for every year that the vehicle is on the road.
The amount of VED is also split into three groups. First year (FYR), standard rate (SR) & the premium supplement (PS). Therefore an expensive EV, which is classed as a zero emission vehicle would face a zero first year (FYR), a zero standard rate (SR) but a £320 premium supplement (PS).
For cars registered after 31st March 2017, the following rates will be applicable.

Premium rated cars that produce $CO_2$ emissions at 0g/km are taxed £0 (FYR), £0 (SR) & £320 (PS). Premium rated cars that produce $CO_2$ emissions at 1 - 50g/km are taxed £0 (FYR), £135 (SR) & £320 (PS). Premium rated cars that produce $CO_2$ emissions at 51 - 75g/km are taxed £15 (FYR), £135 (SR) & £320 (PS). Premium rated cars that produce $CO_2$ emissions at 76 - 90g/km are taxed £100 (FYR), £135 (SR) & £320 (PS). Premium rated cars that produce $CO_2$ emissions at 91 - 100g/km are taxed £120 (FYR), £135 (SR) & £320 (PS). Premium rated cars that produce $CO_2$ emissions at 101 - 110g/km are taxed £140 (FYR), £135 (SR) & £320 (PS).

For cars that were registered before 1st April 2017, the following rates are applicable.

Cars that produce $CO_2$ emissions at 0g/km are taxed £0 (FYR), £0 (SR) & the PS is not applicable. Cars that produce $CO_2$ emissions at 1 - 100g/km are taxed £0 (FYR), £0 (SR) & the PS is not applicable. Cars that produce $CO_2$ emissions at 101 - 110g/km are taxed £10 (FYR), £10 (SR) & the PS is not applicable.

Despite EV's being zero emission vehicles, the VED must be applied for every year. Failure to apply could result in the vehicle being classed as un-taxed, which will result in fines being applied to the registered owner. Also, as a Tesla costs more than £40,000 they are classed as premium vehicles despite being zero emission vehicles, therefore as they are exempt from paying £0 in the first year (FYR) & £0 for every subsequent year (SR), they are eligible to pay £320 every year due to the premium supplement (PS).

As the number of EV's on the road increases, the government will change the VED to compensate for their tax losses (not only from VED, but also from the 57.95p fuel duty they receive from every litre of petrol & diesel). The VED will therefore always fluctuate & it is important that all vehicle owners keep themselves appraised on the current level of VED that applies to their vehicles.

## Salary sacrifice

Salary sacrifice enables employees to sacrifice some of their gross salary in order to receive the benefit of driving an EV as a company car. Because the sacrifice is executed before tax & National Insurance contributions are applied, employees effectively save money in the acquisition of their new car in a similar way that other savings such as childcare, gym membership or cycle-to-work schemes operate.

This scheme is also available for all vehicles that emit 75g/km of $CO_2$ or less, therefore the scheme can also be used for hybrids.

From a company's perspective, the scheme provides an opportunity for organisations to offer employees a brand new, fully maintained EV at a lower cost than they could achieve in the retail market in a tax efficient way. The company may also benefit from reduced National Insurance contribution payments from the scheme.

However, as the UK tax laws are constantly subject to change & are in addition extremely complex, it is important that independent advice is obtained if the scheme is used to buy a vehicle.

## Reduction in BiK tax for company car drivers

Company car tax is designed to encourage employers & company car drivers to choose cars with lower levels of $CO_2$ emissions. Therefore the incentives are offered both to the company & to the recipient of the vehicle. The company car tax payable by an employee is based on the vehicle P11D value which is multiplied by the appropriate BiK rate (this is determined by the g/km of $CO_2$ emissions & the fuel type) & the employee's income tax rate providing significant savings over high $CO_2$ emitting vehicles.

EV's currently offer the lowest BiK rate of any fuel type. Since the Autumn 2017 Budget, the UK Government confirmed that any charging provided by an employer to an employee in the workplace is not considered a benefit-in-kind, but as the UK tax laws are constantly subject to change & are in addition extremely complex, it is important that independent advice is obtained if the scheme is used to buy a vehicle.

## 100% First year allowance (FYA)

Expenditure on company cars is not eligible for annual investment allowance, but by opting for a new low emission car, it is still possible to achieve a 100% deduction against profits in year one. The vehicles that this FYA applies to are the same as the ones that the UK Government has recently defined as Ultra Low Emission Vehicles (ULEV). These are vehicles which have $CO_2$ emissions below 50g/km, or are electrically powered. The same vehicles that qualify for a 100% discount on the London Congestion Charge.

The other current requirement is that the vehicle must be purchased before 31st March 2021 to qualify (but this deadline may be extended) & if the vehicle is used for both business & private use, the first-year allowance must be reduced proportionately to reflect the amount of private use.
In addition to the FYA for the vehicles, it is also possible for business' to also claim 100% FYA for any expenditure incurred on installing electric charge-point equipment. This benefit will expire on 31st March 2023 for Corporation Tax purposes & on 5th April 2023 for Income Tax purposes.

## Approved mileage allowance payments (AMAPs)

If an employee uses their EV for business purposes, then AMAPs will apply in the same way as for petrol or diesel cars. That is: Any reimbursement by the employer for his/her business mileage is tax & NIC free provided it is no higher than the AMAP rates. The HMRC has advised that the fuel rate for electricity is 4p per mile. Any reimbursements in excess of the AMAP rate is taxable & must therefore be reported to HMRC.

If the employer reimburses at a rate lower than the AMAP rate, the employee can claim 'mileage allowance relief' (MAR). An employee may receive a taxable benefit in connection with their personal electric car if their employer: pays for a vehicle charging point to be installed at the employee's home, provides a charge card to allow access to commercial or local authority vehicle charging point or pays to lease a battery for the employee's car. Up to 5$^{th}$ April 2018, only if an employer provides electricity to charge the employee's car.

In each case, the taxable benefit will be calculated in the usual way & based on the cost to the employer. However, as the UK tax laws are constantly subject to change & are in addition extremely complex, it is important that independent advice is obtained if the scheme is used to buy a vehicle.

# EEC

The EEC has been promoting efficient vehicles since their Directive 2009/33/EC of the European Parliament & of the Council of 23$^{rd}$ April 2009 on the promotion of clean & energy-efficient road transport vehicles & also from their Directive 2006/32/EC of the European Parliament & of the Council of 5$^{th}$ April 2006 on energy end-use efficiency & energy services. These documents allow their members to utilise whatever incentives & directives as they see fit. So far, 15 of the 27 EEC members provide tax incentives for electrically chargeable vehicles & 17 countries levy $CO_2$ related taxes on passenger cars.

### Austria

All EV's are exempt from the fuel consumption tax which is paid on the first registration of the vehicle & also from the monthly vehicle tax.

In addition to these tax breaks, hybrid vehicles & other recognised alternative fuel vehicles benefit from a fuel consumption tax that pays a bonus to passenger cars that have a low $CO_2$ emission.

Alternative fuel vehicles which include hybrids can qualify for as much as €800 in annual bonuses. As of January 2016, pure EV's also qualify for a deduction of the VAT (Value-Added Tax) from the purchase price of a new EV.

## Belgium

Until 31$^{st}$ December 2012, a personal income tax deduction of 30% was levied from the purchase price including VAT for all new EV's, up to €9,190. Hybrids were not eligible in that scheme. Currently, there is a tax deduction up to 40% for investments in external recharging stations that are publicly accessible, up to a maximum of €250.

Brussels is now committed to banning all ICE diesel vehicles in the city by 2030. They also have a policy that allows free transport on subway, trams, busses & shared bikes on high pollution days.

## Bulgaria

All EV's including cars, motorbikes & mopeds are exempt from their annual circulation tax.

## Cyprus

All vehicles with emissions less than 120g/km of $CO_2$ are exempt from paying registration taxes.

## Czech Republic

All EV's, hybrids & alternative fuel vehicles that are used for business purposes are exempt from their road tax.

## Denmark

In 2016, EV's lost their exemption from registration tax. This is currently being phased back in until 2020. They are also set to introduce a law to ban diesel ICE cars registered after 2018 from entering Copenhagen. They are currently looking into banning the sale of all new petrol & diesel cars starting in 2030, & then a ban on the sale of hybrid cars starting in 2035.

## Estonia

All EV's are exempt from fees incurred in city public parking & EV's are also allowed to use bus lanes.

## Finland

An individual registering a new EV in the period of 1st January 2018 to 30th November 2021 is eligible for a grant of €2,000 providing the purchase price of the EV is €50,000 or less. In addition, there are a growing number of free charge points that are set up in the country by merchants & private individuals. This now makes it feasible to drive an EV, for free from Helsinki through to Sweden & then all the way to Copenhagen.

## France

Since 1st January 2008 France has used a bonus/penalty system that offers a financial incentive, for the purchase of any cars that have low carbon emissions & also a financial disincentive on the purchases of high emission vehicles.

From 1st January 2017 there was a €10,000 bonus for scrapping a diesel vehicle that was over 10 years-old, whilst currently there is a bonus for purchasers of an EV which is set at €6,000 & also a scrapping bonus of €4,000. The French government are currently intending to introduce a new bonus for any two-wheeled EV's, but the level of the incentive has not yet been published.

The financial penalty system is set to increase the fee for vehicles that emit more than 191 g/km up to €10,000. Currently, there is a €1,000 purchase bonus for plug-in hybrids with $CO_2$ emissions set between 21- 60g/km & the current purchase bonus for non-rechargeable hybrids is set to be stopped at some point in the foreseeable future.

In 2017 they announced that they will ban sales of all new petrol & diesel ICE vehicles by 2040 & Paris is now committed to banning all ICE diesel vehicles from the city by 2024 & all other ICE vehicles by 2030. At present, cars made prior to 1997 are banned from Paris on weekdays & plans are in place to make certain streets EV only zones by 2020. Also, the first Sunday of every month sees a complete car ban between 10am – 6pm (exceptions are made for delivery vehicles & taxis) in the urban centres (1,2,3 & 4 *arondissements*).

At present, there is a clean air zone system that operates in certain areas of France. Cities include Paris, Lyon, Grenoble, Lille, Strasbourg, Toulouse, Chambery & Marseille. Other areas include the Department of Gironde, Department of Bouches-du-Rhône, Department of Hérault, Department of Savoie, Department of Isère, Department of Vendée, Department of Eure-et-Loir & Department of Puy-de-Dôme.

In all these departments & cities it is mandatory to have a '*Crit'Air vignettes*' (badge) displayed on the front window of the vehicle. There are six different coloured badges, each of which denotes the level of pollution that the vehicle emits. 'Crit'Air 1' is for electric & hydrogen-powered vehicles, which is the cleanest group, through to dark grey/black 'Crit'Air 6' which is for mostly older, diesel cars & these are the dirtiest.

These Crit'Air badges allow or restrict access to permanent low emission zones (known as ZCR's (*zone à circulation restreinte*)) & temporary emergency low emission zones (known as ZPA's (*zones de protection de l'air*)).

ZCR's do not let certain polluting vehicles (based on their Crit'Air sticker) into the zone at any time, whilst the ones that are allowed in have to display the window badge to show their emissions & will risk a fine if they do not have one. ZPA's are slightly different as they will only ban certain vehicles (based on their Crit'Air badge) when the location is at risk of dangerously-high levels of air pollution & you will still receive a fine of you do not have a sticker displayed at all times.

The ZPA's operate by temporarily banning Crit'Air 6 vehicles when the pollution reaches a certain level. If the pollution gets worse, they then ban Crit'Air 5 vehicles, & so on until the only vehicles allowed on the roads are Crit'Air 1 vehicles. Any vehicle driving in France is expected to comply. Fines of €68 & €135 have been set for non-compliant vehicles driving without stickers & for those who are driving where they shouldn't, therefore if you are planning to drive your vehicle in France, it is important that you apply for a '*Crit'Air vignettes*' for your vehicle before you go.

## Germany

The German government has created an initiative to develop Germany into a leading market for electric mobility which it calls 'Nationale Plattform Elektromobilität' (NPE). The aim of this initiative is to get 1 million electric vehicles on German roads by 2020. Also, the government will not provide subsidies for the sales of EV's but will fund research in the area of electric mobility.

Currently, EV's & PHEV's are exempt from the annual circulation tax for a period of five years from the date of the vehicle's first registration.

Since February 2016, the German government offers €5000 new EV subsidy, but the car industry is to cover 40% of the cost of this purchase subsidy. Private buyers would get the full €5000 subsidy, while corporate buyers would receive €3000 for each electric car & the program is expected to run until 2020. After this date, the incentives will fall by €500 a year. As of 1st September 2016 there were 26 EV's & hybrid cars & vans that were eligible for this purchase bonus.

In 2016 they announced that they will ban sales of all new petrol & diesel ICE vehicles by 2030. In September 2018 a German court ordered the City of Frankfurt to ban all diesel vehicles (except those manufactured after 2015) from the city. The following month, the same court ordered Berlin to implement the same ban. Hamburg has introduced a ban on older diesel vehicles on two main roads in the city.

### Greece

As of 1st July 2016 onwards the registration tax for EV & hybrids was reduced to 50%. Athens is now committed to banning all ICE diesel vehicles in the city by 2025.

### Hungary

All EV & hybrids are exempt from registration tax & the Government announced that from 27th October 2016, all EV's would be eligible for a 21% rebate of the gross purchase price & this rebate is capped at 1,500,000 Ft. In addition, to promote EV's, the Government has added some other regulatory incentives, such as green license plates & simplified tax & regulations on electric charge points.

## Iceland

All EV's are exempt from VAT up to Íkr 6,000,000 & the tax is applied at the normal rate for the remainder of the purchase price. EV's also get free parking in the city centre for up to 90 minutes & this benefit also applies to cars with $CO_2$ emissions which are less than 120g/km & weigh less than 1,200 kg.

## Ireland

Until December 2012, all EV's were exempt from the vehicle registration tax (VRT). The exemption was then replaced by a €5,000 credit against the tax. Currently, the annual motor tax for EV's is set at €120.

ESB eCar operate the national network of charging points in Ireland. This network is free to use with an RFID card provided by the company to all EV owners who wish to use this network. The sustainable energy authority of Ireland now offers a government grant of up to €5,000 for the purchase of a new EV. EV registration tax has now been waived & EV owners pay the lowest rate of annual road tax, which is based on emissions. Finally, the first 2,000 electric cars registered in Ireland are also eligible for the installation of a free home-charging point worth about €1,000.

Under their 'Project Ireland 2040', they announced that they will ban sales of all new petrol & diesel ICE vehicles by 2045.

## Italy

EV's are exempt from the annual circulation tax or ownership tax for five years from the date of their first registration, after which the EV's benefit from a 75% reduction of the tax rate applied to an equivalent ICE powered vehicle.

Also, buyers of EV's & any vehicle that emits 70g/km or less of $CO_2$ are eligible to receive from €1,500 to €6,000 rebate.

Rome has recently announced plans to ban all diesel vehicles from Rome by 2024. Milan has also announced a series of measures too, where they propose to ban older diesel ICE vehicles from the city during weekdays.

## Latvia

Every single EV including cars, goods vehicles, buses & motorcycles are exempt from payment of the Vehicle Operation Tax.

## Luxembourg

Currently, anyone buying an EV or PHEV will receive a subsidy which provides a €5,000 refund on the purchase of a new 100% EV & €2,500 for a PHEV that has a $CO_2$ emission of 50g/kg or less. Refunds of €500 are also on offer for the purchase of an electric quad, motorcycle, light motorcycle (125 cm3) or moped (& pedelec 45). The actual refund is 25% of the cost, excluding VAT of the vehicle, but does not exceed €500.

Buyers of hydrogen fuel cell cars & vans are also eligible for the €5,000 refund. These subsidies cover vehicles which enter service from 1st January 2019 to 31st December 2019 & have not been registered in another country. Also, a subsidy of up to €300 will be offered on the purchase of a new electric bike or pedelec25 (pedal-assisted bike with a power output of no more than 0.25kW) purchased in 2019.

## Monaco

Purchasers of EV's & PHEV's are now eligible to receive €9,000 from the Monegasque Government. Also, these vehicles are allowed to park for free at any public parking facility.

## Netherlands

The Dutch government has set a goal of obtaining 1 million vehicles on their roads by 2025. As such they set incentives such as total exemption of the registration fee & exemption from road taxes, which has resulted in savings of approximately €5,324 for private car owners over four years & €19,000 for corporate owners over a five year period. Hybrids were also exempted from these taxes if they emitted less than 95 g/km for diesel ICE vehicles, or less than 110 g/km for petrol ICE vehicles. These incentives have now finished & instead have been replaced by a system where all EV's pay a 4% registration fee whilst PHEV's pay a 7% fee. The government also offers a €3,000 subsidy on the purchase of EV taxis or delivery vans. This is increased to €5,000 per vehicle in Amsterdam, Rotterdam, The Hague, Utrecht & The Arnhem-Nijmegen metropolitan area.

In Amsterdam EV owners also have access to parking spaces reserved for EV's along with free charging points. EV owners in Rotterdam are entitled to one year of free parking in the city centre & also access to subsidies of up to €1,450 if they chose to install a home charger that uses green electricity.

In 2017 they announced that they are looking into banning sales of all new petrol & diesel ICE vehicles by 2030.

## Norway

Currently, the existing incentives are that EV's are exempt in Norway from all non-recurring vehicle fees, including purchase taxes, which are extremely high for ordinary cars & also 25% VAT on the purchase price, which make the EV purchase price competitive with conventional cars. All EV's are also exempt from the annual road tax & toll payments. They are also permitted to use the bus lanes.

Their tax system levies higher taxes on heavier vehicles. Therefore plug-in hybrids are more expensive than similar conventional cars because of the extra weight of the battery & the additional electric components. Since 1st July 2013, the existing weight allowance for conventional hybrids & PHEV's of 10% will be increased to 15%.

In 2016 they announced that they will ban the sale of all petrol & diesel vehicles by 2025. Currently the city of Oslo are implementing restrictions, which includes restricting access to privately owned vehicles, creating pedestrian walkways & reducing the amount of parking spaces within the city. The aim for Oslo is to have the city car free by 2020.

## Portugal

EV's are fully exempt from both the Vehicle Tax due upon purchase (*Imposto Sobre Veículos*) & the annual Circulation Tax (*Imposto Único de Circulação*). Personal income tax provides an allowance of €803 upon the purchase of an EV. EV's are also exempt from the 5 - 10% company car tax rate which is part of the Corporation Income Tax.

They also offered a subsidy of €5,000 for the first 5,000 new EV's sold in the country. In addition to this, there is also a €1,500 incentive if the consumer turns in a used car as part of a down payment for a new EV.

## Romania

Since April 2011 the government has offered a grant of up to 25% of the price (up to a maximum of €5,000) for the purchase of a new EV. They also offer a scrapping scheme where anyone who wishes to purchase an EV will receive vouchers of over €5,000 in return for their used car.

With regard to hybrid vehicles, with or without plug-in capabilities, a €550 grant is offered, plus an additional €160 grant for hybrid vehicles emitting under 100g/km of $CO_2$. Combined with the scrapping scheme the total grant can be up to €2,200. EV & hybrid vehicles are both exempt from the environmental tax which also acts as a registration tax. As of March 2015 EV's are also exempt from the annual tax, whilst hybrid vehicles have a 95% reduction.

Currently, the grant has increased to €10,000 for the purchase of an EV & car owners will also receive an additional €1,400 if they end their registration of a car that is older than eight years old.

## Spain

In 2011, the government introduced incentives that included direct subsidies for the purchase of new EV's for up to 25% of the purchase price before tax. Up to a maximum of €6,000 per vehicle. In addition, they also offered 25% of the gross purchase price of other electric vehicles such as buses & vans up to a maximum of €15,000 or €30,000, depending on the range & type of vehicle. Madrid is now committed to banning all ICE diesel vehicles in the city by 2025. They have already restricted access to petrol ICE vehicles made prior to 2000 & diesel ICE vehicles made prior to 2006. After 2020, these older ICE vehicles will not be permitted to enter the city at all.

## Sweden

From January 2012 the government provided a subsidy of 40,000 kr per car for the purchase of EV's & other 'green cars' with ultra-low carbon emissions below 50g/km of $CO_2$, along with an exemption from annual circulation tax for the first five years from the date of the vehicles first registration. This was for owners of EV's with an energy consumption of 37 kWh per 100 km or less & also hybrid vehicles with $CO_2$ emissions of 120g/km or lower.

Following a high take up of the scheme by 2016 it was adapted so that only zero emissions cars were to be entitled to receive the full 40,000 kr premium, whilst other green cars & PHEV's would receive half of this subsidy. The exemption for the first five years of ownership from the annual circulation tax is still in place.

They are currently looking into a system that is similar to France. That is a bonus/penalty system that offers a financial incentive for the purchase of low carbon emission vehicles & a financial disincentive on the purchases of high emission vehicles.

## Canada

In 2010, the Ontario Ministry of Transportation (MTO) created the Electric & Hydrogen Vehicle Incentive Program (EHVIP). To qualify under this scheme, EV's & PHEV's had to be purchased or leased from a seller in Ontario & owned or leased for at least 12 months. 12 month term leased vehicles received 33% of the total incentive, 24 month term leased vehicles received 66% of the total incentive & 36 month term leased vehicles received 100% of the incentive.

Vehicles also had to be on a government list of approved vehicles & cost less than CA$75,000. EV's with a battery size of 5 - 16kWh were eligible for a cash incentive ranging between CA$6,000 - CA$10,000. EV's with a battery size greater than 16kWh qualified for a cash incentive ranging between CA$9,000 - CA$13,000 & any vehicles with five or more seats were eligible for an additional CA$1,000. However this scheme has now been cancelled.

Currently, EV's & PHEV's in Ontario are now eligible for green license plates which allow them to be driven in the province's high-occupancy vehicle toll lanes at no cost, regardless of the number of passengers in the vehicle.

On 1st January 2012 Quebec started to offer a rebate of CA$8,000 for new EV's equipped with a minimum of 4kWh battery & a CA$1,000 rebate for hybrids. Businesses are eligible for a 75% rebate on installation costs up to CA$5,000 for charging stations. A 50% rebate is also available for individuals to install home charging stations, up to a maximum of CA$1,000. They also intend to install charging stations on their Electric Circuit route, 1,000 near government buildings & plan to electrify their vehicle fleet with EV's & PHEV's.

Since 2018, new zero emission vehicle legislation came into effect that obliges any car manufacturer who sells more than 4,500 new vehicles per year over a three-year average in the province of Quebec, to sell their customers a minimum number of EV's & PHEV's. Therefore 3.5% of the total number of cars sold by car dealerships in Quebec now has to be 'zero emissions vehicles' (ZEV). The percentage rises to 15.5% in 2020. They have also introduced a credit system that allows car manufacturers to pay for credits that allow them to make up the difference if they fail to meet their EV or PHEV quotas. Since 2015 In British Columbia, they have British Columbia's clean energy vehicle (CEV) program which offers an incentive valued at CA$5,000 for EV's with a minimum of 15kWh battery capacity, & CA$2,500 for a PHEV or extended range vehicle with a smaller battery (minimum of 4kWh capacity) & even CA$6,000 for hydrogen fuel cell vehicles. They also offer a "SCRAP-IT" program that offers incentives for scrapping ICE cars from the year 2000 or earlier. Also, just like Ontario, British Columbia's EV & PHEV's owners can apply for a special decal which allows access to their high-occupancy vehicle lanes regardless of the number of passengers in the vehicle.

# USA

President Barack Obama set the goal for the US to become the first country to have one million EV's on their roads by 2015. To help facilitate this, a range of incentives were introduced, but despite the incentives, Obama's goal is unlikely to be achieved until well into 2020. This is likely due to the low cost of petrol & diesel at the US pumps. Also, the initiatives that were offered are now quickly reaching the date which the tax incentives that were offered will expire.

Currently the tax credit for new EV's is worth $2,500 plus $417 for each kilowatt-hour of battery capacity over 4 kWh up to a maximum battery payout of $5,000. Therefore, the maximum amount of the credit allowed for a new EV is $7,500. Both the Nissan LEAF & the Chevrolet Volt PHEV are eligible for the maximum $7,500 tax credit. Any EV produced after 2010 are now eligible for an IRS tax credit from $2,500 - $7,500, but as time progresses, the tax credits available will reduce. Tax credits for individuals & business' to create charge points were also introduced, but all these credits have now ceased.

Individual states are free to create their own schemes & California is one such state that has opted to do so & now offer rebates on approved EV's. This may have contributed to the fact the 40% of the US' EV's & PHEV's are in California. Also, any vehicles that meet the specified emissions standards may also be issued with a Clean Air Vehicle (CAV) decal that allows the vehicle to be operated by a single occupant in California's high-occupancy vehicle lanes (HOV), or carpool or diamond lanes. All EV's are classified as federal inherently low emission vehicles (ILEV's) & therefore are entitled to these white CAV stickers.

Since November 2014, 37 states have created incentives & tax exemptions for EV's & PHEV's, along with utility-rate breaks & other non-monetary incentives such as free parking & HOV lane access. Also, EV's & PHEV's in all states are now eligible for the $7,500 income tax credit.

## Australia

The federal government currently offers no incentives for EV ownership & imposes a substantial financial disincentive with a Federal Luxury Car Tax (LCT) that is applied on all new vehicles valued over a certain threshold (2014 – 2015 this was set at A$61,884). The application threshold for this tax is increased to A$75,375 for fuel efficient vehicles, which they define as vehicles with a fuel consumption rating under 7 litres per 100 kilometres.

However, as the state & territory governments are responsible for motor vehicle registrations, two have offered incentives or rebates for EV's. In Victoria, EV's & PHEV's receive a A$100 annual discount on their vehicle registration & in the 'Australian capital territory', they have reduced the stamp duty on any motor vehicle purchases to A$0 that has 'zero tailpipe emissions', therefore every EV is eligible for this discount.

## Japan

They have been providing provided subsidies & tax discounts on the purchase of EV's, natural gas ICE powered vehicles, methanol ICE powered vehicles & PHEV's since 1998. They currently offer tax deductions & exemptions for what they call 'environmentally friendly & fuel efficient vehicles'. The criteria are set according to an environmental performance criteria & these requirements are applied equally to both foreign & domestic produced vehicles. It provides purchasing subsidies for consumers purchasing a new passenger car without a trade-in & consumers buying a new car who are trading in a used car that was registered 13 years ago or earlier.

# China

The Chinese government have decided that only EV's & PHEV's are subject to their new purchase incentives. On 1st June 2010, the Chinese government announced a trial program to provide incentives up to 60,000 Yuan for private purchases of new EV's & 50,000 Yuan for PHEV's in the cities of Shanghai, Shenzhen, Hangzhou, Hefei & Changchun. These subsidies are paid directly to the vehicle manufacturers, not the vehicle buyers, but the government expects that the vehicle prices will be reduced to take account of this 'rebate'.

Over subsequent years, the Chinese government has redesigned & reinvented their incentives many times. They introduced a credit based system, where each car manufacturer who produces more than 30,000 vehicles each year must comply with some new rules, where they get credits for the EV's & hybrids they produce. These credits are granted by the fuel efficiency & weight of the vehicles, therefore more fuel efficient vehicles count for more credits. Credits equate to rebates. Range has now also been added into the credit formula & EV incentives for cars with at least 400 km of range has increased from 44,000 Yuan to 50,000 Yuan, whilst vehicles with less than 150 km range have now been removed from the list of vehicles that qualifying for the rebate.

Currently, they incentivise the vehicle manufacturer's to push & sell their EV & hybrid vehicles, rather than provide incentives for the vehicle purchasers.

# Chapter 9 – **Maintenance**

Despite the fact that an EV is a far simpler machine than any ICE powered vehicle, you can not escape the fact that it will need scheduled & unscheduled maintenance. This is true for all ICE powered vehicles as well as all EV's & PHEV's. If you own or have ever owned an ICE powered vehicle you will be aware that these periods of maintenance will crop up from time to time, especially if you have, or have had older models. You will also be painfully aware that these maintenance issues can be a painful expense.

However, as was previously stated, currently in the UK only 1% of the mechanics are trained to work on EV's & hybrids, so the chances of getting your local garage to work on an EV or hybrid may be problematic & this may force you to use the dealership where the EV or hybrid originated, which will inflate the costs. So what can an EV or hybrid owner do to reduce these costs?

First, the obvious answer is to do what you can yourself. But obviously, as the risk of electrocution is a real threat to life, it is vitally important that you only undertake what is safe, never tamper with the electrics, electronics or the battery.

# Minor maintenance

## Brakes

An EV or hybrid will most likely have brake disks & brake pads at the front of the vehicle. These can also be found on ICE powered vehicles too, so any local garage or tyre/brake franchise will be able to maintain & replace these items when they become worn. You may even be competent to do so yourself.

The good news is that unlike an ICE powered vehicle, an EV or hybrid also uses regenerative braking, & therefore there will never be as much wear on the brake disks or pads. They could even last twice as long because the electric motor acts as a brake. The conventional disk & pad brakes are there to make up the difference & to operate if there is no electrical power. Therefore there is a positive effect on the brakes. Also, there may also be disks & pads at the rear wheels, or even drum brakes. The drum brakes also double as the parking brakes, but if the EV or hybrid has two electric motors, the layout will be the same as at the front.

## Tyres

Obviously an EV or hybrid has tyres just like an ICE powered vehicle, but one thing worth considering is that every EV & hybrid is much heavier than a comparable ICE vehicle, so it is important to check the tyres regularly. The tyres may not last quite as long as those on an ICE vehicle because an EV or hybrid will always produce more torque & the additional weight will also add to the wear.

Again any local garage or tyre/brake franchise will be able to maintain & replace the tyres when they become worn. They are no different to any other tyres.

## Coolant system

All EV's & hybrids will have a coolant system that cools the electronics & the batteries. These systems will occasionally need to be topped up with coolant. This will be a simple matter where the reservoir is filled in exactly the same way as you would for adding windscreen washer fluid.

The exact type of coolant & where to fill the reservoir will be detailed in the vehicle's owner manual. Any local garage will be able to top up the coolant when it needs topping up, but you may feel competent to do so yourself.

## Wiper blades

There is absolutely no difference to the wiper blades on an EV, a hybrid or an ICE vehicle. Replacing wiper blades is one of the most simple maintenance tasks that can be undertaken on a vehicle, but as with the previous items, if you do not feel confident changing the blades, any local garage will be able to undertake this task for you.

## Headlamps & bulbs

Again, there is absolutely no difference to the headlamps & the bulbs on an EV, a hybrid or an ICE vehicle. Replacing bulbs that have blown is one of the most simple maintenance tasks that can be undertaken on a vehicle, but as with the previous item, if you do not feel confident changing the bulbs, any local garage will be able to undertake this task for you.

## Fluids

Besides the coolant fluid which was dealt with on the previous page, there are two other fluids that are present in an EV or hybrid. They are brake fluid & windscreen washer fluid. The brake fluid should be checked & replaced as instructed in the vehicle's owner manual. The windscreen washer fluid should be added periodically, as per the instructions in the vehicle's owner manual.

Any local garage will be able to top up the fluids when they need topping up, but you may feel competent to do this task for yourself. Any other fluids, if present, are sealed & therefore should not be easily accessible.

## Motor factor parts

All the above items can be sourced at your local motor factors, along with steering & suspension components that will be specific for your EV, but the majority of the components for the vehicle will be what is known as a 'dealer only part'. Those are components that are only available at the dealership.

With regard to a hybrid, the majority of the components will be available at a motor factors as the hybrid will have an ICE engine & it is just an regular ICE vehicle with a battery & electric motor thrown in. The parts that will not be available are those components that are hybrid specific such as the electronics, the electric motor & the battery. Those components will be the dealer only parts.

# Major maintenance

As well as the minor maintenance items that will need to be taken care of, there is also a major maintenance issue that must also be addressed. However, this need not be a burden, so long as you follow the procedure that is detailed in the vehicle's owner manual. However, there will come a point in time when the battery will be beyond its useful life & will need to be replaced.

## Battery system

The one maintenance area that proves to be problematic in an EV or hybrid is the battery system. As EV's & hybrids can use nickel-metal-hydride (NiMH), lithium-ion (Li-Ion) or similar batteries, it should now be clear that they all have a limited & useful lifespan. All batteries will lose some efficiency over time & if the car is kept long enough, the battery will need to be replaced before it becomes unusable or unsafe.

Most EV/hybrid manufacturers provide a battery warranty to cover the battery pack & sometimes any related components for several years or 100,000 miles, whichever comes first. The exact time span, mileage & other details will be dependant on the manufacturer. If the battery pack needs to be replaced outside the warranty period, it will prove to be a very expensive undertaking.

Although second hand batteries are available for EV's & hybrids from online auction sites, it could prove to be a false economy to purchase & fit one of these as there will be no guarantee & no information to how they were cared for during their previous life. This is therefore one item that will need to be sourced & fitted by the vehicle manufacturer's dealership. By buying direct, the battery may also have a warranty & hopefully be fitted correctly.

It is in the owner's interest to care for the battery by following the charging regime that will be found in the vehicle's owner manual. Using incorrect charging methods could degrade, damage or destroy the battery, therefore it is in the owner's interest to ensure that battery maintenance & charging is undertaken in the manner described. Looking after the battery should be the number one concern if you wish to have a prolonged period of electric motoring, rather than a dangerous fire &/or explosion.

## Servicing

Servicing your EV or PHEV is something that should prolong the life of your vehicle. Due to the fact that the mechanics that are trained to service EV's & PHEV's tend to be found at the dealerships, it would be advisable to book your vehicle in for a service at the dealership.

A local garage may turn you away if you ask to service your EV or PHEV there, so you may not have any option but to use the services of the dealership.

The trained mechanics should be fully versed in your vehicle & therefore should be able to advise you on what work will need to be undertaken to prolong the lifespan of your vehicle. One downside to using a dealership is that the costs will be greater than it would be at a local garage, however this extra cost will be offset; as having a full service history which includes the dealers stamp will always add value to your vehicle when you decide to sell it. It is also good practice to time your service to coincide with just before having an annual MOT.

# The UK MOT

Many countries in the world have annual or bi-annual tests which are meant to ensure that the vehicle is safe to drive & therefore it acts as a test to the road worthiness of the vehicle. In the UK it is called a 'ministry of transport test' (MOT) & is undertaken on all vehicles that reach three years old & every subsequent year after that. Without it the vehicle's insurance is not valid & it is un-taxable. Therefore to ensure the vehicle is street legal, it must pass an annual MOT. Only goods vehicles powered by electricity that were registered before 1$^{st}$ March 2015 are exempt from the MOT.

Therefore all EV's & PHEV's (cars & vans) are eligible for MOT's, just as any other vehicle in the UK. EV's are exempt from the 'emissions test' element of the test, but they are not exempt from the remainder of the MOT.

All garages who display a government MOT sign are registered with the government & approved to issue MOT's. Part of their licence conditions (given by the UK government) is that they can not refuse to undertake an MOT on any vehicle. Therefore if an EV is presented to a garage for an MOT, they must undertake the MOT, despite the fact that in all probability there is no-one in the garage that is trained in EV's.

The Motor Vehicles (Tests) Regulations 1981 (which is the Act that defines which vehicles can be refused & why) does not allow 'not having a mechanic qualified in EV's' as an excuse to refuse a MOT. The governments own advice to MOT testers states "You can't refuse to carry out an MOT test on one of these vehicles because you're not familiar with them. You need to know how to safely drive the vehicle & immobilise it. If you're unfamiliar with the vehicle type, ask the customer to explain: the starting & moving off procedure, how to make the vehicle safe".

The governmental advice to MOT testers also goes on to state that "all electrically powered vehicles pose a theoretical risk because of the very high voltage used in these vehicles. The voltages in these vehicles are usually between 350 volts & 600 volts. These are lethal levels". Also, regarding pacemakers, the MOT tester is told to "consult your doctor before working with these vehicles".

In a MOT, the headlight alignment & brightness will be examined, along with all other light functions, which include hazard lights, indicators & brake lights. Seatbelts, windscreen wipers, the windscreen itself is examined for chips & cracks, the horn, washer fluid & all other components of the car will be tested, just as with a petrol car. This also includes aspects such as mirrors, electrics & the air filter. Failure with any of these components will cause an overall MOT test failure, just like an ICE vehicle.

Another part of the test will be an inspection for signs of rust or corrosion. This will be performed all over the vehicle, under the bonnet, around the body, even on the underside, which is why the vehicle is raised off the ground. The chassis, suspension components, brakes & mounting points will also be examined, but the MOT tester is not permitted to remove any part of the vehicle to check for rust. Most electric vehicles are fitted with a panel underneath, so this will be kept in place throughout the test. Any corrosion to the underside of the EV may therefore not be visible.

In addition to the above, the wheel alignment & steering checks are undertaken, along with a visual inspection of the tyres & the wheels themselves. The brakes, suspension & wheel bearings are also checked for wear & tear. The wheels are examined to make sure nothing is impeding them from spinning freely, or exerting any undue pressure or friction.

# Maintenance & service costs

There will always be costs associated with maintaining & servicing any vehicle. That is to keep them running & to keep them road legal, but just how much can it cost?
Below are some comparable costs (obtained from KeeResources) for various ICE powered vehicles & their EV equivalent over a 4 year/60,000 mile servicing regime.
The BMW 1-Series (ICE powered) 118d SS sport 150dpf would cost £2,929.94, whilst the BMW i3 (EV) Electric Drive Loft Professional Media 170bhp would cost £2,264.05 over the same period, which is a saving of £665.89 for the EV over the ICE.

The Hyundai IONIQ (PHEV) Plug in Hybrid Premium SE 120PS would cost £2,120.88, whilst the Hyundai IONIQ (EV) Electric Premium SE 120PS would be £1,543.20 over the same period, which is saving of £577.68 for the EV over the PHEV.

A Kia Soul (ICE) GDI 132bhp would cost £1,570.86, whilst the Kia Soul (EV) Electric EV 109PS would be £1,203.57 for the same time period, which is a saving of £367.29 for the EV over the ICE.

The Nissan Pulsar (ICE) Tekna XTRONIC DIG-T SS 115PS would cost £2,298. 63 & the Nissan LEAF (EV) Tekna 30kW Electric 109PS would cost £1,538.62 which makes a saving of £660.01 for the EV over the ICE.

The Renault Clio (ICE) Signature Nav EDC Tce SS 120bhp would cost £2,114.31 to maintain, whilst the Renault ZOE (EV) i Signature Nav Rapid Charge 41kWh Electric 88PS would cost £1,169.96 which is a saving for the EV of £944.35 over the ICE.

Therefore the maintenance costs appear to be considerably cheaper for the EV over comparable ICE powered vehicles.

However, the amount saved over an 8 - 10 year period would not cover the cost of a new battery pack. This is all due to the fact that a typical Li-Ion battery used in an EV is estimated to be good for more than 100,000 miles, but after this the range will become noticeably shorter & the battery will need more & more charging whilst giving less & less range.

Currently it would cost between £10,000 - £5,450 to replace the battery in a Nissan LEAF (40kWh), or approximately £3,000 - £2,000 for a reconditioned second hand battery. Over a 10 year period, assuming that the battery needed replacing after 10 years, the amount saved from the servicing would only be £1,650.25. If the LEAF's battery were leased at £129 per month, this would add an additional £15,480 (on top of £3,846.55 for 10 years servicing) but maintaining the ICE Pulsar would be just £5,746.58 over 10 years, so despite the fact that EV's are being advertised as costing less to maintain, in reality the ICE powered vehicles work out to be far cheaper to maintain. It is a simple case of the government & EV manufacturers manipulating the data just to make the EV's appear cheaper to run, even when they are not.

# Table of illustrations

The cover illustration is copyright to P Xavier (2019).

Figure 1 Extractable energy from various fuels per kilo (P Xavier © 2019) ............................................................................. 14

Figure 2 Tesla Model S 85kWh battery pack (Public Domain Image 2019) ............................................................................. 61

Figure 3 Close up of the Tesla Model S battery (Public Domain Image 2019) ................................................................................. 62

Figure 4 Batteries connected with a series connection (P Xavier 2017) ... 63

Figure 5 Batteries connected with a parallel connection (P Xavier 2017) . 64

Figure 6 How the parts fit together (P Xavier © 2019) ................................ 69

Figure 7 The AC family tree (P Xavier © 2019) ........................................... 70

Figure 8 The DC family tree (P Xavier © 2019) ........................................... 75

Figure 9 DC electricity viewed in an oscilloscope (P Xavier © 2017) ........ 83

Figure 10 AC electricity viewed in an oscilloscope (P Xavier © 2017) ...... 83

Figure 11 Worldwide AC/DC standards (Public Domain Image © 2006) .. 85

Figure 12 Three phase AC current (P Xavier © 2017) ................................ 86

# About The Author

Mr Xavier is in his 40's & currently living in the South of England. He is desperately trying to make a living, live a good life, learn to play the ukulele, grow a rather splendid handlebar moustache & decide what to have for dinner tonight. With his other hand he's trying frantically to learn another language whilst also planning the next chapter of his life.

This & all his other books are available online from reputable ebook retailers.

Manufactured by Amazon.ca
Bolton, ON